PRINCIPALS
TEACHING
the LAW

*To school principals and those
who promote legal literacy with their teachers.*

PRINCIPALS
TEACHING
the LAW

10
Legal Lessons
Your Teachers
Must Know

DAVID SCHIMMEL
SUZANNE ECKES
MATTHEW MILITELLO

CORWIN
A SAGE Company

For information:

Corwin
A SAGE Company
2455 Teller Road
Thousand Oaks, California 91320
(800) 233-9936
Fax: (800) 417-2466
www.corwin.com

SAGE Ltd.
1 Oliver's Yard
55 City Road
London EC1Y 1SP
United Kingdom

SAGE Pvt. Ltd.
B 1/I 1 Mohan Cooperative
    Industrial Area
Mathura Road,
    New Delhi 110 044
India

SAGE Asia-Pacific Pte. Ltd.
33 Pekin Street #02-01
Far East Square
Singapore 048763

Printed in the United States of America

Library of Congress Cataloging-in-Publication Data

Schimmel, David.
Principals teaching the law : 10 legal lessons your teachers must know /
David M. Schimmel, Suzanne E. Eckes, Matthew C. Militello ; foreword by Jon Manier.
    p. cm.
Includes bibliographical references and index.
ISBN 978-1-4129-7223-9 (pbk.)
    1. School principals—Legal status, laws, etc.—United States. 2. Educational law and legislation—United States. 3. Liability for school accidents—United States.
4. Educational leadership—United States. I. Militello, Matthew. II. Eckes, Suzanne.
III. Title.

KF4133.S34 2010
344.73'07—dc22   2010007248

This book is printed on acid-free paper.

10   11   12   13   14   10   9   8   7   6   5   4   3   2   1

Acquisitions Editor:	Arnis Burvikovs
Associate Editor:	Desirée A. Bartlett
Editorial Assistant:	Kimberly Greenberg
Production Editor:	Veronica Stapleton
Copy Editor:	Adam Dunham
Typesetter:	C&M Digitals (P) Ltd.
Proofreader:	Wendy Jo Dymond
Indexer:	Molly Hall
Cover Designer:	Scott Van Atta

Contents

Additional materials and resources related to *Principals Teaching the Law: 10 Legal Lessons Your Teachers Must Know* can be found at www.corwin.com/teachinglaw

Foreword

Like many of you reading this book, I too have been a school principal. Because of this, I know the incredible demands you encounter every day. First, you're expected to create a professional learning environment where all students demonstrate success. To get there, you have to maintain order, hire and retain a high-quality staff, build partnerships with your community, monitor effective instruction, and create professional development opportunities. However, after nearly 20 years in school leadership, I have learned a valuable, and occasionally painful, lesson: *School educators need to know school law.* I have also learned that educators expect the principal to know and advise their staff on issues pertaining to school law. In a society that has become increasingly litigious, a solid understanding of basic principles of school law is not only necessary, but it may also save your job.

School-leadership and teacher-preparation programs continue to provide a mixed bag of legal knowledge for future educators. As a result, we must consider this uncomfortable reality: *School leaders that have limited knowledge of school law are giving advice to faculty members who are often misinformed about school law.* Regardless of their training, school leaders have a professional and moral responsibility to ensure that their institutions abide by the legal standards set in legislation and case law.

As a school leader, I have always believed that I am the chief teaching and learning officer. Therefore, my solution to the school law dilemma has been to sign up for workshops, classes, and trainings. Inevitably, when I returned home and began sharing my learning, I'd struggle to re-create the presentations. After all, I wasn't the expert presenter. In fact, I sometimes wondered if I was doing more harm than good by presenting information that was too legalistic or perhaps inaccurate.

Principals Teaching the Law: 10 Legal Lessons Your Teachers Must Know provides school leaders with both reliable content *and* tools to deliver the content. Teaching teachers is a difficult task. Educators know quality instruction, and they are critical consumers of learning activities. Fortunately, this book provides important and timely lessons utilizing strong instructional components. Each lesson includes clearly stated goals, a warm-up activity, clearly written school-law content, an application activity, and an assessment measure. It is my experience that when you provide these lessons, your audience will quickly engage, discussions will bloom, and topics will reach beyond the initial learning session. Once you provide a lesson, you'll be able to infuse the lesson's ideas into weekly meetings, faculty communications, and daily conversations.

As a principal, I see this tool being a stalwart in your professional toolbox. Present the lessons at faculty meetings either on a regular basis or as specific issues arise. Several years ago, as a high school administrator, I was faced with the challenge of a student group that wanted to distribute an "underground" student newspaper. I had faculty members who openly supported the students. I had faculty members who demanded the students be disciplined. How did I know what the "right" decision would be? Chapter 2, Student Freedom of Expression, contains information that would have helped me make a sound decision. More importantly, the collaborative-learning activities in Chapter 2 would have provided me a vehicle to facilitate a group lesson.

As a central-office administrator, I now provide advice to school principals on a regular basis. In providing counsel, I often consider our district's legal responsibility as a filter. Frequently, I find myself reaching for *Principals Teaching the Law* because it brings key ideas to the surface quickly and in ways that are clearly understood.

While writing this forward, I was contacted by one of my elementary school principals. The principal needed to address parental concerns regarding playground supervision. I directed the principal to review the information in Chapter 1, Liability for Student Injuries, prior to making a final decision on his response. Having a new understanding of his legal responsibility for playground supervision, the principal is now able to properly direct his playground supervisors, resulting in a safer environment for all children at his school.

Similarly, a new principal recently expressed to me concern regarding his knowledge of the implementation of individual education programs (IEPs). While the principal was a veteran teacher and quite competent in many aspects of his new role, the background information provided in Chapter 3, Special Education, provided him a quickly accessible reference to key legal principles. Not only did the principal develop his personal understanding, he also believed that sharing these lessons would profoundly change the behavior of his teachers. In particular, the scripted example of an IEP dramatically outlines how educators, armed with information about special education law, can avoid common mistakes and better protect the rights of their students and their parents.

In a world where information on individuals is accessible like never before, having school employees understand the potential consequences of their "personal" behavior is critical. As part of our new-teacher induction programming, I plan to present the Chapter 7 lesson, Teacher Lifestyle Choices and Out-Of-School Conduct, collaboratively with the president of our teacher's union. I believe the joint presentation, along with the poignant examples from the lesson, will provide our new teachers a powerful message on professional behavior.

Frankly, *Principals Teaching the Law: 10 Legal Lessons Your Teachers Must Know* may not eliminate the need for specialized legal advocacy. However, I believe this book will provide the school principal with timely, important legal content and the means to deliver the content in an effective manner. Teachers will leave your meetings with new knowledge that will allow you to focus their efforts on their teaching and the learning needs of their students.

Jon Manier, School Administrator,
Farmington, Michigan

Preface

A recent national survey revealed that the vast majority of teachers have taken no course in school law in their pre- or inservice programs and that their principals are their primary law teachers (Schimmel & Militello, 2007). The survey also indicated that most teachers were uninformed or misinformed about the rights of students and teachers, and most principals give their faculty legal advice in an incomplete and unsystematic fashion. This ad hoc advice is often ambiguous, confusing, and sometimes misleading. Interestingly, there are no books about school law designed to enable principals to be conscious, informed, and effective school-law teachers for their staffs. Further, research demonstrates that teachers consider the study of legal issues to be one of the most essential areas of teacher preparation. The purpose of this book is to meet this critical unmet need: to provide school principals with the lesson plans they need to incorporate school law into their inservice programs and thus enable their teachers to become legally literate practitioners of preventative law.

What we know is this: School principals are uniquely situated to be the chief purveyor of legal information in school for their teachers. However, we also know that current school principals do not feel they have the content knowledge or the mechanisms to help their teachers. What they need is a tool and further knowledge. We believe that when equipped with the right tool and the right knowledge, they can make teaching school law an ongoing and integral part of their work. This book provides both the tool and the necessary knowledge for school principals to become effective teachers of school law for their staffs.

REFERENCE

Schimmel, D., & Militello, M. (2007). Legal literacy for teachers: A neglected responsibility. *Harvard Educational Review, 77*(3), 257–284.

Acknowledgments

Our students inspired this work. Current teachers and administrators that we help train have commonalities: the desire to improve student outcomes and the need to remove law as a barrier to their important work. Hearing these struggles, we have conducted a number of studies highlighting case law and educators' knowledge. Doing this work led us to an obvious conclusion: School leaders need guidance to help them alleviate the strains school law too often presses upon them.

This work would not have been possible without the assistance and critique of a number of people. In particular, we would like to acknowledge those who have assisted us in conducting our research, including Janet Decker, Jake Eberwein, Susan Giullian, Roland Joyal, J. D. LaRock, Kelly Rapp, and Emily Richardson.

We also want to thank those who took the time to read and comment on early drafts of this book. We are especially grateful for the thoughtful and thorough comments provided by Sarah Burke (school psychologist in Stoughton, Wisconsin), Jon Manier (administrator in Farmington, Michigan), and Gina Umpstead (assistant professor at Central Michigan University). We also want to thank some of our students who piloted a number of the lessons, including The Advanced School Law Course (A615) at Indiana University and Law for School Leaders at the University of Massachusetts, Amherst.

Finally, we want to thank our families, who have inspired our work and allowed us to focus on this book:

Christopher and Ian Shaw

Elizabeth, Dominic, Luke, and Gabriel Militello

Barbara Schimmel

PUBLISHER'S ACKNOWLEDGMENTS

Additionally, Corwin gratefully acknowledges the contributions of the following reviewers:

Robert L. Blake, Principal
Mainland Regional High School
Linwood, NJ

Jim Howard, Clinical Associate Professor
Washington State University
Spokane, WA

Mark O. Kelly, Principal
Malibu High School
Malibu, CA

Neil MacNeill, Principal
Ellenbrook Primary School
Ellenbrook, Australia

Alice L. Manus, Assistant Principal
Soldan International Studies High School
St. Louis, MO

Cathy Patterson, Former Assistant Principal
Walnut Unified School District
Walnut, CA

Bonnie Tryon, Principal for Instructional Planning and Support
Cobleskill-Richmondville Central Schools
Cobleskill, NY

Darryl Williams, Principal
Montgomery Blair High School
Montgomery County Public Schools
Silver Spring, MD

About the Authors

David Schimmel is a professor of education at the University of Massachusetts, Amherst, and a visiting professor at Harvard University's Graduate School of Education. He is the author of over 60 articles and the coauthor of six books about law and education, including *Teachers and the Law* (2007, 7th edition) and *School Law: What Every Educator Should Know* (2008), and is recipient of the Education Press Association of America's Distinguished Achievement Award for Excellence in Educational Journalism. After graduating from Yale Law School, he briefly practiced law, was an Army Infantry Officer, and served on the Peace Corps staff for six years before starting his teaching career at UMass. His current research and writing focuses on promoting legal literacy for teachers.

Suzanne Eckes is an associate professor in the Educational Leadership and Policy Studies Department at Indiana University. Suzanne has published over 60 school-law articles and book chapters, is an editor of the *Principal's Legal Handbook*, and is a member of the board of directors for the Education Law Association. She is the recipient of the Jack A. Culbertson Award for outstanding achievements in education from the University Council of Educational Administration. Prior to joining the faculty at Indiana University, Suzanne was a high school French teacher and an attorney. She earned her Master's in Education from Harvard University and her law degree and PhD from the University of Wisconsin-Madison.

Matthew Militello is an assistant professor in the Leadership Policy and Adult and Higher Education Departments at North Carolina State University. He held a similar position at the University of Massachusetts, Amherst, where he was also the educational administration program coordinator. Prior to his academic career, Militello was a middle and high school teacher, an assistant principal, and a principal. His research focuses on developing principals' knowledge and skills in the areas of school law, school data, and collective leadership. Militello has more than 30 publications, including articles in *Educational Policy, Education and Urban Society, Harvard Educational Review, Journal of School Leadership, Leadership Quarterly, Principal Leadership,* and *Teachers College Record.* Militello also coauthored another Corwin book, *Leading With Inquiry and Action: How Principals Improve Teaching and Learning* (2009). He received his undergraduate degree and teaching certification from the University of Michigan and his MEd and PhD from Michigan State University.

Introduction and Overview

How the Principal Can

Be the Chief Law Instructor: 10 Lesson Plans

The goal of this book is to enable principals to become better-informed and effective school-law teachers. Although teaching law is not in their job description, principals already *are* the chief law teachers in their schools. This is because most principals frequently give legal advice—in staff meetings, in informal conversations, and in the way they develop, interpret, and enforce school rules. While this legal advice is often appropriate, there are many times when it is confusing, misleading, incomplete, and even incorrect. This advice (or lack of advice) often leads to two types of mistakes by teachers: (1) failing to take disciplinary action when they should and (2) unintentionally violating students' rights when they should not.

RESULTS OF LEGAL ILLITERACY

First, the failure to act is often the result of oversimplified administrative warnings. According to a national survey (Schimmel & Militello, 2007), the most frequent legal advice principals give to teachers is "Don't touch students." Because of this and other "thou shall nots," many teachers view law as a source of anxiety and fear. Thus, an elementary teacher reported that he does not break up fights among his third graders because he's afraid that if he does, and a student is injured, he could be sued in court, disciplined by his principal, or both. This widespread belief among teachers that *any* touching of students involves inherent legal dangers persists despite the fact that it is always legal and appropriate for teachers to use reasonable force to protect their students and themselves.

1

Second, because the vast majority of teachers have taken no course in school law in their pre- or inservice programs, they are not aware that they function as agents of the government and are therefore restrained by the Bill of Rights. As a result, teachers may unintentionally violate students' Constitutional rights when they require them to stand for the Pledge of Allegiance, search their backpacks for possible contraband without reasonable suspicion, or punish them for statements in class or on T-shirts because they might offend someone.

Teachers' lack of awareness of students' rights can cause friction, frustration, and possible litigation. This was illustrated by a high school principal who explained, "Although I haven't had any major lawsuits, it's the legal misunderstandings with students, parents, and teachers that take up much of my time." For example, she told about one of her teachers who sent a student to her office to be suspended for refusing to take off an "offensive" T-shirt that said that President Bush was an "International Terrorist." As the principal knew the student had a First Amendment right to wear the shirt because it caused no disruption, she refused to suspend him. As a result, the teacher felt embarrassed and unsupported by her principal. On the other hand, if the principal had "supported" her teacher and suspended the student, this might have led to a conflict with the parents and a possible lawsuit—which the school would have lost.

In sum, legally illiterate teachers may fail to take appropriate action—ignoring misbehavior, permitting disruptions, or rescinding discipline because of meritless threats by parents or students. In addition, when teachers are unaware of how the Bill of Rights protects students, they may unintentionally violate students' rights regarding free speech, due process, or search and seizure. These negative consequences of legal illiteracy are compounded by the fact that most teachers get much of their legal advice from other teachers who are similarly uninformed or misinformed.

BENEFITS OF LEGAL LITERACY

If principals teach the basic principles of school law as a regular part of their teachers' professional development program, there can be a number of positive results. For example, when teachers understand the laws that govern discipline and the reasonable use of force, they will not be afraid to break up a fight because of unfounded fears that they could be held personally liable if a student is injured, nor will they fear a lawsuit if they put a restraining hand on the shoulder of a second grader who is constantly jumping out of his seat, disrupting the class, and likely to injure himself.

Furthermore, if public school teachers understand that they are agents of the government and are therefore constrained by the Constitution, they are likely to think and consult with their principal before they search a student or demand that a student take off a controversial political T-shirt because they fear it might offend someone.

When principals become effective law teachers, their staffs will get the information about school law from knowledgeable sources—not from the rumors and myths from the Teachers' Lounge School of Law. As practitioners of preventive law, teachers will know when to consult with informed administrators. By having a legally literate staff, principals will benefit because of fewer legal mistakes and misunderstandings by teachers. This should reduce the time and energy principals now have to devote to teachers' legal confusions and to preventable parental complaints, threats, and possible litigation—freeing the principal to focus on quality teaching and learning. Thus, there are multiple benefits of having a legally literate staff. We have written this book to help principals make this happen.

With this information, teachers will no longer see themselves as potential victims of the law. Instead, they will be able, in a constructive sense, to "take the law into their own hands." As a result, they also will be able, in partnership with their principal, to uphold the law with confidence and feel empowered to protect their students, their school, and themselves.

WHO CAN USE THIS BOOK

We do not presume the user of this book has an advanced knowledge of school law. Rather, we presume the users wants to provide themselves and their colleagues with a basic knowledge of school law so that the law does not hamper their ability to be an effective educator. Therefore, we see a number of users for this book:

- *Current principals* seeking ways to remove legal issues as barriers to teaching and learning in their schools
- *Aspiring principals* seeking knowledge they will need to lead the schools of tomorrow
- *Current teachers* seeking answers to common concerns about what to do when confronted with legal situations
- *Superintendents* working directly with their principals
- *Instructors in teacher- and principal-preparation programs* seeking a practical guide to preventative school law

- *District administrators* seeking content for new-teacher orientation and extended-day and summer professional development opportunities
- *School board members* who need to be knowledgeable of school-law issues (e.g., in Massachusetts, board members are required by law to attend an orientation that includes school law)
- *Other school personnel* (e.g., guidance counselors, paraprofessionals, bus drivers, school security and resource officers) who also confront legal issues in schools

HOW WE ORGANIZED THE BOOK

We selected 10 lesson plans to present in this book. While other topic areas could have certainly been included, we selected these 10 lessons on the basis of our research that has highlighted the most frequent or common questions schoolteachers and principals ask about school law. We also used topics that are timely and relevant. That is, we often included cases that have been highly publicized by the media and the courts. Table 0.1 summarizes the 10 law topics we selected.

Table 0.1 Summary of Topics

Lesson Plan	Questions Answered
1. Liability for Student Injuries	When can teachers be held liable for student injuries that occur in their classrooms or when they are on duty in the hallways or playgrounds? If they leave their classrooms unattended, would they always be held liable for injuries that occur? Can teachers be held liable if a student is injured when they break up a fight or drive a student in their car? Can they restrain a disruptive student? Are there state or federal laws that protect teachers against being held liable? Does insurance or parental waivers protect them? Does a teacher's duty of care vary with the age of the student?
2. Student Freedom of Expression	What is the scope and limits of student freedom of expression in the public schools? Can teachers prohibit messages on student T-shirts that are controversial, offensive, or vulgar? Can schools prohibit students from distributing unapproved newspapers or flyers on campus? Can students be punished for messages on their Web sites that insult teachers, criticize school policies, or might cause disruption?

paper copies

Lesson Plan	Description
3. Special Education	When is a student entitled to special rights under IDEA (Individuals with Disabilities Act) and under Section 504 of the Rehabilitation Act of 1973? What constitutes a free appropriate public education under IDEA? What is required in an IEP (individualized education program)? Do all teachers have responsibilities to implement IEPs? What is meant by "the least restrictive environment" and "related services"? What "reasonable accommodations" must be made under Section 504?
4. Student Due Process and Search and Seizure	Are students entitled to due process before a short suspension? If so, what process is due? What procedural rights do they have before being expelled? What is an adequate notice and hearing? When are they entitled to a lawyer, to bring witnesses, to cross-examine their accuser or to appeal? Is due process different for students in special education? When can students be searched?
5. Student Harassment and Bullying	When can schools be held liable for sexual harassment among students? Do students have to tell teachers or principals about the harassment? Does the harassment have to be severe or pervasive? Do schools have a duty to prevent the harassment? Does the harassment have to be sexual? What about harassment based on religion, race, or sexual orientation? When are schools liable for a teacher's harassment of a student?
6. Teacher Freedom of Expression	Can teachers be punished for publicly criticizing school policy or for complaining about working conditions? Do whistle-blower laws protect teachers? Do teachers have a right to use controversial materials or methods in class? Do they have a right to express their personal views about political or social questions in response to student questions?
7. Teacher Lifestyle Choices and Out-of-School Conduct	Can administrators discipline teachers for immoral or unprofessional conduct away from school? What constitutes immoral or unprofessional conduct? Can teachers date students if they are over 18 and not in their classes? What illegal conduct would justify firing a teacher? Could photos on Facebook get teachers in trouble?
8. Religion	Are students allowed to pray before, during, or after school? Must schools recognize student prayer clubs? Are invocations and benedictions permitted at graduation? What about silent prayer or meditation? Are courses that teach

(Continued)

(Continued)

Lesson Plan	Description
	about the Bible or religion permitted? Must schools excuse students from reading books or studying topics that violate their religious beliefs? Are Christmas assemblies OK? Do teachers have a right to exclude evolution or include intelligent design in their science curriculum? Can students be required to stand for the Pledge of Allegiance?
9. Student Records: The Family Educational Rights and Privacy Act	Are parents entitled to see all of their child's records? Can parents prohibit outsiders from having access? Are there circumstances that allow the records to be shared without parental consent? Do noncustodial parents have a right to see their child's records? Are parents entitled to a hearing to challenge the accuracy of their child's records or grades? Do teachers have a right to see the records of their students? Can parents sue teachers for putting negative and critical comments in the student's records?
10. Abuse and Neglect	What constitutes abuse or neglect? Are all school staff required to report child abuse? To whom must educators report? Must teachers be sure of abuse before reporting? If an investigation determines that no abuse occurred, could parents sue the reporting teacher for defamation?

HOW TO USE THIS BOOK

We have designed each lesson so that it can be completed in one 60-minute professional development session. These are "ready-made" lessons that require a minimum of preparation time for the presenter. We fully realize that this target may not be achievable if the user is seeking a comprehensive understanding of the law for the participants. Therefore, we include a number of alternative ideas and supplemental resources, so users can add to the lessons as they see fit. For example, we provide strategies that ask participants to prepare for the law lesson prior to entry in the professional development session.

We have designed these lessons around principles of good teaching and learning. However, we strongly encourage the presenters to use ideas from other lessons (e.g., using the motivator strategy in the teacher-freedom-of-expression lesson plan with the content of the religion lesson) or proven strategies from their own professional experience (e.g., group activities that you have found valuable) throughout these lesson plans. Our lessons are divided into the following steps:

1. Activator/Motivator

We agree with John Dewey (1902) and many cognitive psychologists that learning occurs through the heart on the way to the mind. As such, we created an anticipatory set—what we call an Activator/Motivator—for each lesson. Each Activator/Motivator is designed to garner the attention of participants and engage their hearts and minds. Each Activator/Motivator can be modified to meet the specific context in your local school setting.

2. Rationale/Objectives

Learners need to know what they are expected to learn. For each lesson, we have identified the purpose and specific goals. Also in each lesson, we suggest that the goals should be posted and stated. However, each facilitator should integrate the goals into the lesson as they see fit.

3. The Law

We provide current, relevant legal content for each lesson. However, this book is not designed as a comprehensive educational-law text. Instead, it provides a summary of the basic legal principles that are most important for teachers to understand. We do not advise that facilitators read The Law section to participants or simply hand out this section for participant review. In order to promote a learner-centered pedagogical approach, we offer a specific teaching and learning strategy for each lesson. Each is designed to be ready to use; however, as with the Activator/Motivator, we encourage facilitators to modify lessons and to replicate pedagogical strategies from other lessons as they see fit.

4. Application of Content to Practice

Principals will use a variety of activities with teachers to help them apply what they learned in the legal-content section to real school issues.

5. Assessment

The big questions in any teaching setting are, Did they learn? and Can they apply the knowledge? The purpose of this section is to ascertain learning. Finally, as with the other lesson plan sections, we highly recommend setting (e.g., elementary or secondary) and personal modifications (e.g., emphasizing certain aspects of a lesson).

We also provide two additional sections for each lesson:

Questions and Answers

We predict that participants will have additional questions as a result of the lessons. While there is no end to the "What if . . ." questions, we provide a list of questions teachers are likely to ask. The questions can also be integrated into many aspects of each lesson, including the Activator/Motivator, The Law, or the Assessment.

Resources and Materials

We have provided a set of resources, materials, and references at the end of each chapter.

Relevant Quotes Historical and/or precedent-setting quotes and cases are highlighted. These can be used for multiple purposes in different parts of the lesson plans.

Materials All the material needed to conduct each lesson will be listed for each lesson. We also provide details regarding the use of technologies, such as converting YouTube clips to computer files that can be accessed in a meeting without Internet connectivity.

References A list of readily available references will be provided. Rather than a comprehensive list, we identify specific chapters of popular school-law texts that can be used to augment each lesson.

Features of the Lesson Plans

We use seven features throughout the book to guide the facilitators for each portion of the lesson plan. Throughout each chapter, you will see these features as you flow through the various elements of each lesson.

Icons

We provide four icons to assist the facilitator. The first is a *clock* that signifies the amount of time that should be spent on each section in order *to complete the lesson in 60 minutes.* Another icon will signify that the

Figure 0.1

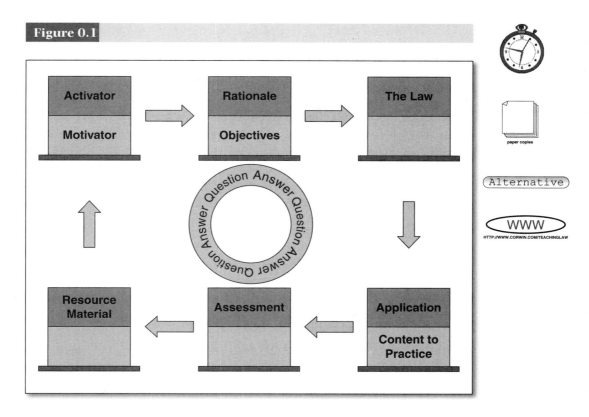

following content can be *reproduced* (photocopy, overhead transparency, or content used to develop a presentation slide to be used with a computer and an LCD projector). An icon will also be used to highlight an *alternative activity.* Finally, an icon will signify a web link that can be accessed at www.corwin.com/teachinglaw.

Figure 0.2

CAUTIONARY NOTE

It is important to acknowledge two issues associated with the delivery of the school-law lesson plans. First, we fully understand the difficulty of teaching, especially teaching adult learners. That is to say, any presentation can easily go astray with "what if . . ." questions. We anticipate that many teachers may want to debate the merits, realities, or "correctness" of the law discussed in these lessons. If facilitators are restricted to 60-minutes sessions, they need to stress that these lessons are not designed as debates but rather to present what educators need to know to protect themselves, so they are not inhibited by misinformation. Facilitators should anticipate this and, if possible, build in a small amount of time (preferably before the lesson) for participants to opine about the law itself.

Second, although we believe this book is accurate at the time of publication, it is not intended to be used as legal advice for anyone facing or contemplating litigation. Because the law is constantly changing and varies among the states, educators considering legal action should not rely on this book. Instead, they should consult with a knowledgeable lawyer and/or their professional association. As litigation is often an unhappy, expensive, difficult, and time-consuming experience, going to court should usually be a last resort. Therefore, we hope this book will enable teachers and principals to resolve disputes through discussion, negotiation, and education rather than litigation.

REQUEST TO USERS

This is a pioneering book. We believe it is the first of its kind, and we want it to work for you and your teachers. By sending us your comments and suggestions, you can help us improve the next edition. What did you find useful? What should be added or eliminated? What was confusing or unclear? Please send your comments and suggestions to David Schimmel, University of Massachusetts (schimmel@educ.umass.edu), Suzanne Eckes, Indiana University (seckes@indiana.edu), and Matthew Militello, North Carolina State University (matt_militello@ncsu.edu).

Thanks from each of us.

References

Dewey, J. (1902). *The child and curriculum.* Chicago: University of Chicago Press.
Schimmel, D., & Militello, M. (2007). Legal literacy for teachers: A neglected responsibility. *Harvard Educational Review, 77*(2), 257–284.

How the Principal Can Be the Chief Law Instructor

10 Lesson Plans

Liability for Student Injuries

1

Protecting Your Teachers, Your Students, and Your School

BACKGROUND ON THE ISSUE

Probably no area of school law arouses more anxiety, confusion, and misunderstanding than the possibility of being sued for student injury. Rumors circulate in many teachers' rooms about educators who have lost their jobs and their life savings because some injured student won a million-dollar award against them. As a result of the possibility of being sued, many educators view the law as an invisible monster hiding in every classroom, hallway, and playground ready to ensnare any teacher who makes an innocent mistake. Thus, there emerges a sense that teaching is an especially dangerous profession in which hazards are greater, liability is more personal, negligence more likely, and the result of negligence more disastrous for educators than other people. One result of this erroneous perception is that many teachers fail to discipline students when they should because of unfounded fear of being sued. Similarly, some teachers don't intervene in fights when they may, or if they do, they worry unnecessarily about being sued if a student is injured.

This lesson will clarify many of these confusions and misunderstandings. It will outline what an injured student has to prove to hold teachers or schools liable for their injuries. One outcome of this lesson is that it will enable teachers and administrators to have a common understanding of the law that applies to student injuries and will enable them to collaborate in practicing preventive law. As practitioners of preventive law, educators will be able to protect themselves, their students, and their schools.

Activator

Motivator

10 min

In this activity, ask participants to indicate whether they think educators can be held liable for student injuries in a number of hypothetical cases. Distribute copies of Table 1.1, and ask teachers to indicate if they believe the teacher in each case would be held liable. If you choose, you may tally totals for each response and write the number in each column. Finally, tell participants that you will return to these cases later in the lesson, and transition into the rationale and goals of the lesson.

Table 1.1   Liability Hypothetical Cases

paper copies

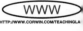
HTTP://WWW.CORWIN.COM/TEACHINGLA

Hypothetical Cases	Is the Teacher Liable?		
Case 1. As a result of Mr. Big's using reasonable force to break up a fight in the hallway, one of the students hits his head on the floor and has a serious concussion.	Yes	No	Don't Know
Totals			
Case 2. After a play rehearsal, Mrs. Care gives a student a ride home without parental permission, and the student is injured, but not because of the teacher's negligence.	Yes	No	Don't Know
Totals			
Case 3. Although Mr. Carefree is supposed to be on duty in the gym at 1 p.m., he drinks another cup of coffee in the teachers' room and then walks into the gym at 1:15. At 1:14, a high school student was seriously injured when he bumped heads with a classmate while jumping for a rebound during a friendly basketball game.	Yes	No	Don't Know
Totals			

Hypothetical Cases	Is the Teacher Liable?		
Case 4. Ms. Busy leaves her class for 10 minutes to duplicate science worksheets. She tells the students to work quietly while she is gone. When she leaves, some students begin to throw spitballs, pencils, and paper planes. After 6 or 7 minutes, a girl is struck by a pencil and blinded in one eye.	Yes	No	Don't Know
Totals			
Case 5. As the bus was leaving the high school on a field trip, 16-year-old Flo Friendly suddenly reached out of the window to waive at a friend and broke her arm when it hit a lamppost. She sued teacher Tripper for failing to adequately supervise and for not warning students not to open the bus windows.	Yes	No	Don't Know
Totals			
Case 6. Instead of paying attention to the students when she was on playground duty, Mrs. Lesscare was gossiping with another teacher. During this time, Sue Sadly ran across the playground, tripped, fell on her face, broke three teeth, and received six stitches.	Yes	No	Don't Know
Totals			
Case 7. Despite repeated warnings to Bob Bobbing to stay in his seat, he continued to jump out of his seat, disrupt the class, and perhaps injure himself. As a result, teacher Strictman put a restraining hand on Bob's shoulder—against the advice of a colleague who told him, "Never touch a student."	Yes	No	Don't Know
Totals			

Alternative

Consider sending the scenarios out beforehand. That way, you can ask teachers to complete all of the scenarios without taking time out of the lesson.

Rationale

Objectives

Rationale

3 min

Because there is widespread fear of being held liable for student injury (which may inhibit appropriate disciplinary action) and because of extensive misunderstanding about how the law applies to these situations, it is important for teachers to understand when and why educators can and cannot be held personally liable.

Objectives

• Post and/or state the following objectives for the lesson plan:

1. Teachers will identify what an injured student must prove in order to hold teachers and/or schools liable.

2. Teachers will be able to apply the "reasonably prudent teacher" standard in order to practice preventive law.

3. Teachers will become familiar with how insurance, as well as state and federal laws, might protect educators from personal liability.

The Law

15 min

In this section of the lesson plan, the principal will provide the content needed for educators to make informed and legal decisions. This lesson is based on the law of torts. *Torts* are civil (as contrasted with criminal) wrongs and are primarily an area of state law, rather than law made by the federal government. Tort law imposes a *duty of care* on educators. This means that educators must use *reasonable care* not to injure their students and to protect their students from *foreseeable dangers.* If educators fail to use reasonable care, they are considered *negligent.* If their negligence is the *cause* of a student's injury, they or their school may be held liable in monetary *damages* to compensate the student for his or her injuries. To determine whether an educator is negligent, courts ask if the educator acted as a *reasonably prudent teacher* (RPT) should have acted under the circumstances. If in doubt about how a RPT should act, a teacher should *consult* with prudent, experienced teachers and administrators who have faced similar circumstances.

In considering whether to hold teachers and/or schools liable for a student's injuries, judges would apply the above principles and ask four questions. (Use Table 1.2 as a handout or presentation slide to provide the law for each of these questions.)

Table 1.2   Student Liability Questions and Legal Principals

HTTP://WWW.CORWIN.COM/TEACHINGLAW

Question	The Law
1. Was there a duty of care?	Educators have a duty not to injure their students and to protect them from known or foreseeable dangers.
2. Was there negligence?	Teachers are negligent when they fail to act as a hypothetical *reasonably prudent teacher* (RPT) should have acted under the circumstances. To determine whether a teacher acted as an RPT, the teacher's behavior is measured against the professional norms of prudent teachers. If they do act as an RPT under the circumstances, they are not negligent. When circumstances are more dangerous (e.g., on field trips, in chemistry class, or when working with young children), an RPT should provide clearer warnings to and closer supervision of students.
3. Did the negligence cause the injury?	The plaintiff (or injured student) must prove not only that the defendant teacher who is being sued is negligent but also that the negligence caused the injury. (Plaintiffs usually sue for a dollar amount for medical expenses, lost wages, and/or pain and suffering to compensate them for their injury.)
4. Was there contributory negligence?	Adults and most high school students are expected to exercise ordinary/reasonable care and not to expose themselves to known or obvious dangers. Therefore, in most states, if an injured person's own negligence contributed to her injury,

(Continued)

Question	The Law
	courts would usually reduce the amount of the dollar award to the injured person in proportion to her negligence. This is known as *comparative negligence.* For example, an older student might have her award reduced by 40% if the judge concluded that she was 40% responsible for her own injury. However, if she was primarily responsible for her injury (i.e., more than 50%), she would probably receive no award. In all states, different standards apply to children. Generally, children under the age of 7 cannot be charged with contributory negligence. Children between 7 and 14 are usually presumed incapable of contributory negligence. And beyond the age of 14, students are expected to act as reasonably prudent students of their age and maturity should act under the circumstances.

Copyright © 2010 by Corwin. Additional materials and resources related to *Principals Teaching the Law: 10 Legal Lessons Your Teachers Must Know* can be found at http://www.corwin.com/teachinglaw.

Alternative

Consider providing teachers with a blank note sheet with the four questions. Ask the teachers to take notes as you deliver the content.

To summarize, the legal principles relevant to student injury—that educators have a duty to act with reasonable care, that they are negligent if they fail to do so, and that they can be held liable if their negligence causes injury—apply in all states The principles are relatively easy to understand, and with practice in applying them, teachers and principals can anticipate and prevent problems that can lead to lawsuits.

Although there is little chance of a reasonably prudent teacher being held personally liable for student injuries, this fact should not make competent teachers less careful. Instead, this knowledge should

1 reduce misinformation and misunderstanding about teacher liability;

2 enable teachers to enforce reasonable discipline and order without unfounded fear; and

3 enable teachers to collaborate with their principals and colleagues in applying the "reasonably prudent teacher" standard to issues of supervision and safety.

As a result of this knowledge, teachers will be less likely to view law as a source of anxiety and instead feel empowered to be practitioners of preventive law when confronting legal issues.

Application

Content to Practice

15 min

Divide the participants into small groups of three to five, and ask them to talk out the hypothetical cases they used in the Activator/Motivator. The goal is to determine whether it is likely that the teachers in the scenarios would or would not be held liable by applying the principles we have explained to the facts of the cases. That is, in each case, ask

1. Was there a duty of care?

2. Was the teacher negligent? That is, did the teacher fail to act as a reasonably prudent teacher should have under the circumstances?

3. Did the teacher's negligence cause the injury?

4. If so, was there contributory negligence that might reduce the award to the plaintiff?

5. After the small groups report the results of their discussion of the cases, the principal can use the answers in Table 1.3 to summarize and clarify how the principles of law would likely apply. The principal may need to address only selective cases, as time permits.

Table 1.3   Application of Principles to Liability Cases

Case Number	Result
1	*Teacher not liable.* Mr. Big has a duty to protect students from being injured. If, pursuant to that duty, he tries to break up a fight and he unintentionally injures a student, he should not be held liable for the student's injury. This is because a teacher who uses reasonable force to protect himself or a student is not negligent even if a student is injured in the process. Furthermore, even if the teacher was negligent, some state laws and the federal Teacher Liability Protection Act (2001) would probably protect him from liability if his action was carried out to "maintain order or control in the classroom."
2	Mrs. Care is *not liable* for the student's injuries if they were not caused by her negligence. The fact that Mrs. Care did not have a parent's permission may or may not have violated a school policy. But even if Mrs. Care did violate school policy (or administrative advice), this would not make her a negligent driver, and if she was not negligent, she cannot be held liable for the student's injury.
3	In this case, Mr. Carefree is *not liable* for the student's injury. By drinking coffee when he should have been supervising the gym, Mr. Carefree was negligent and violated his contractual duties. But, if bumping heads in a friendly game is an accident that would not have been prevented even if a reasonably prudent teacher would have been present, then Mr. Carefree would not be liable for the injury because his negligent absence was not the cause of the accident. Carefree should be disciplined for not being on duty when he should have been supervising the students, but he could only be held liable if the facts of the case were different and the injured student could prove that a teacher's presence would have prevented the injury.
4	Ms. Busy probably is *liable* for the injury of the blinded student. Ms. Busy had a duty to protect her students from injuries caused by other students when such injuries could have been prevented by reasonable supervision. If, under the circumstances of this case, a reasonably prudent teacher would not have left the classroom unattended for 10 minutes, then Ms. Busy was negligent for doing so. And if a reasonably careful teacher would have stopped the students' misconduct before it caused the injury, then a judge or jury could conclude that Ms. Busy's negligence caused the injury.
5	In this case, Mr. Tripper probably would *not be held liable* because a judge or jury would probably conclude that Ms. Friendly was negligent in failing to act as a reasonably prudent high school student should have under the circumstances. High school students have a duty to exercise ordinary care and not to expose themselves to obvious dangers. Even if

Case Number	Result
	Mr. Tripper was not watching Ms. Friendly when she suddenly reached out of the bus, her negligent behavior was the primary cause of the injury—not the action or inaction of Mr. Tripper.
6	Probably *not liable*. Mrs. Lesscare was negligent for not paying attention to the students when she was on playground duty, and perhaps she should be disciplined for her failure to carry out her duty of care. But she could not be liable for the injury to Sue (which was an accident that was caused by her running) if Sue's injury would not have been prevented if Lesscare was carefully supervising and not gossiping.
7	Probably *not liable*. Mr. Strictman may have ignored the advice of his colleagues, but this does not mean he could be held liable for preventing Bob from repeatedly jumping out of his seat, disrupting the class, and possibly injuring himself. Although many educators tell teachers, "Never touch a student," this is overly broad advice and in some situations is poor advice. Certainly, sexual touching of students by teachers is always illegal. But, there are many situations where the law permits teachers to use reasonable force to protect themselves or their students and use reasonable restraint to enforce discipline. In fact, the purpose of the Teacher Liability Protection Act (2001) is to protect teachers from frivolous lawsuits and the fear of liability for their reasonable actions to maintain order in their classrooms.

Copyright © 2010 by Corwin. Additional materials and resources related to *Principals Teaching the Law: 10 Legal Lessons Your Teachers Must Know* can be found at http://www.corwin.com/teachinglaw.

Assessment

7 min

One way to assess teacher understanding is to ask teachers to apply the legal principles they learned to the following variations of the cases we have discussed. Copy Table 1.4, and fold each scenario on the dotted line. Ask participants to read only the question portion of Question 1. Ask participants to pair up and discuss what they each think about the scenario and explain their reasons. After a few minutes, inform the pairs to open their cards and review the answer. Repeat this with the second scenario.

Table 1.4   Student Liability Scenario Flash Cards

Q1. While Mr. Carefree was having coffee instead of supervising the gym, some of the students started a rough basketball game that included pushing, elbowing, and cursing. After 10 minutes of increasingly unsportsmanlike conduct, one of the students intentionally tripped another player who was seriously injured just as Mr. Carefree entered the gym. Is the teacher liable? Why or why not?

A1. Mr. Carefree probably would be held liable because he was negligent in not being on duty in the gym and because a reasonably prudent teacher would have intervened to stop the uncontrolled game before the student was injured.

. . . .

Q2. Just before Ms. Busy returned to her classroom after duplicating worksheets for 10 minutes, a student threw a baseball from the playground that shattered a window and sprayed glass that blinded one student's eye. Is the teacher liable?

A2. Ms. Busy would not be held liable because the presence of a prudent teacher would not have prevented the unforeseeable injury that occurred.

FAQ

As time permits, you may add some of these additional questions to the follow-up discussion.

10 min

1. What should teachers do when they confront new situations that might pose dangers, such as field trips?

When in doubt about what one's duty of care requires, a reasonably prudent teacher should *consult* with other reasonably prudent teachers or administrators who have confronted similar situations. By collaboratively developing and following safety checklists, teachers protect their students, themselves, and their schools.

2. Are teachers liable for *any* injury that occurs if they leave their classroom unattended?

No. There may be emergencies in or outside the classroom that would require a reasonably prudent teacher to *briefly* leave her class, and in these circumstances, she would not be negligent for doing so.

3. Can teachers be held liable for failing to prevent every injury that might occur when they are supervising a class, hallway, or playground?

No. Most injuries are caused by accidents, which are not the result of anyone's negligence and for which no one is liable. Furthermore, teachers cannot be expected to anticipate every situation in which one student could injure another. The law does not expect teachers to prevent unforeseeable injuries, only those that ordinary care can prevent.

4. Do teachers have a duty to physically intervene in a fight?

Not necessarily. It depends on the circumstances. For example, a female teacher has no duty to physically intervene in a fistfight between two high school students and risk injury. In many situations, teachers simply have the duty to seek help when circumstances are beyond their control.

5. What happens if I am injured while breaking up a student fight?

Teachers would be covered by their medical insurance for short- and long-term disability as well as workman's compensation for a serious injury.

6. If parents sign waivers, does that protect teachers and schools from liability?

Not necessarily. In many states, courts construe such waivers very strictly or rule that waivers of responsibility in school activities are against public policy. In a few states, such as Massachusetts, courts uphold waivers in extracurricular activities—especially those that students and parents know are dangerous. Although it is usually wise to ask parents to sign permission slips to permit their children to participate in special activities, parents should not be asked to waive their right to sue educators who are negligent and whose negligence causes student injuries because most courts are not likely to uphold such waivers and because parents should not be asked to waive their children's rights.

7. Are teachers personally liable, or do they have any protections?

Teachers who belong to organizations such as the National Education Association (NEA) or the American Federation of Teachers are provided liability insurance (usually for $1,000,0000) as part of their union dues for negligence claims that might be made against them. This policy costs the NEA less than five dollars per year to insure each member. Because the premium is based on the likelihood of being sued, this indicates that the chances of a teacher being held liable for a student's injury are extremely low. In addition, many school districts and professional associations also provide liability insurance for their employees.

8. What would happen if a student assaulted a teacher?

The student could be subject to school discipline and/or criminal punishment. Although teachers could sue students for damages, this is not likely because even if teachers win their suit, they would be unlikely to collect damages (generally parents are not financially responsible for their children's misbehavior).

(Alternative)

Consider sending a few of these questions to teachers via e-mail, electronic discussion board, or as a hardcopy in their mailbox for them to read and consider between professional development sessions. Responses can then be collected or discussed at the next professional development session.

Resource Material

Relevant Quotes

It is the duty of a school to use ordinary care and to prevent its students from injury resulting from the conduct of other students under circumstances where such conduct would reasonably have been foreseen and could have been prevented by the use of ordinary care. There is no requirement of constant supervision of all the movements of pupils at all times. . . . Children have a known proclivity to act impulsively. . . . It is precisely this lack of mature judgment which makes supervision so vital. The mere presence of the hand of authority and discipline normally is effective to curb this youthful exuberance and to protect children against their own folly.

—Sheehan v. St. Peters Catholic School (1971)

As is often the case, accidents . . . involving school children at play happen so quickly that unless there was direct supervision of every child (which we recognize as being impossible), the accident can be said to be almost impossible to prevent.

—Nash v. Rapides Parish School Board (1975)

Clarifying and limiting the liability of teachers, principals and other school professionals who undertake reasonable actions to maintain order, discipline and an appropriate educational environment is an appropriate subject of federal legislation because the scope of the problems created by the legitimate fears of teachers, principals and other school professionals about frivolous, arbitrary or capricious lawsuits against teachers is of national importance. . . . No teacher in a school shall be liable for harm caused by an act or omission of the teacher on behalf of the school if the actions of the teacher were carried out . . . to control, discipline, expel, or suspend a student or maintain order or control in the classroom or school if . . . the harm was not caused by willful or criminal conduct, gross negligence [or] reckless misconduct.

—Paul D. Coverdell, Teacher Liability Protection Act (2001)

References

Nash v. Rapides Parish School Board, 188 S0.2d 508 (La. 1975).
Sheehan v. St. Peters Catholic School, 188 N.W.2d 868 (Minn. 1971).
Teacher Liability Protection Act, 20 U.S.C. 6731–6769 (2001).

Additional Resources

Alexander, K., & Alexander, M. D. (2009). *American public school law* (7th ed.). Belmont, CA: Wadsworth. (SEE Chapter 11)

Fischer, L., Schimmel, D., & Stellman, L. (2010). *Teachers and the law* (8th ed.). Boston: Allyn and Bacon. (SEE Chapter 5)

Russo, C. (2004). *Reutter's the law of public education* (5th ed.). New York: Foundation Press. (SEE Chapter 8)

Thomas, S., Cambron-McCabe, N., & McCarthy, M. (2009). *Public school law: Teachers' and students' rights* (6th ed.). Boston: Allyn and Bacon. (SEE Chapter 13)

Underwood, J., & Webb, L. D. (2006). *School law for teachers.* Upper Saddle River, NJ: Pearson. (SEE Chapter 6)

Student Freedom of Expression 2

BACKGROUND ON THE ISSUE

Before the 1960s, there was little hope that courts would strike down school rules that restricted student freedom of speech. As a practical matter, the First Amendment did not apply to public schools. This is because courts used a "reasonableness" test to judge school policies. This meant that rules were upheld unless students could prove that they were not reasonable. As administrators could almost always articulate some reason to justify their rules, restrictions on student speech were almost always upheld.

This changed in 1969 when the U.S. Supreme Court handed down a landmark decision in the case of *Tinker v. Des Moines* (1969) that replaced the reasonableness test. In *Tinker,* the Court ruled that the First Amendment applied to students in the public schools, and restrictions on student speech were unconstitutional unless schools had evidence that the expression would cause substantial disruption or interfere with the rights of others.

In the years that followed, the Supreme Court ruled on three other student speech cases that clarified the scope and limits of *Tinker.* In 1986, in *Bethel v. Fraser,* the Court held that lewd and indecent speech is not protected by the First Amendment. In 1988, in *Hazelwood v. Kuhlmeier,* the Court ruled on a school newspaper case and established guidelines on when educators can control school-sponsored student expression. And in 2007, the Court explained, in *Morse v. Frederick,* when schools could restrict student speech that promoted illegal behavior.

These four Supreme Court cases form the constitutional context for today's many controversies about student expression. This lesson will help teachers understand the principles that emerge from these Court decisions. It will also help them understand when they can and cannot restrict such current controversial expressions as provocative T-shirts and offensive Web sites and e-mail messages.

Activator

Motivator

10 min

Distribute copies of Table 2.1, and ask teachers to indicate if they believe that schools violated student freedom of expression in the following cases. If you choose, you may tally total responses by all participants. This can be done individually, or you can post the totals on a slide or overhead. Finally, tell participants that you will return to these cases later in the lesson, and transition into the goals of the lesson.

Alternative

You might enhance the motivator by distributing 3" × 5" cards that say Violation on one side and No Violation on the other side. (Note: This can also be accomplished with color-coded cards. For instance, green would indicate no violation, and red may indicate a violation). Display each T-shirt (see pages 31–32) and ask participants to hold up the card that best expresses how they would rule on the issue.

Alternative

Principals can discuss the contents of a YouTube clip about a student who unfurled a banner that said "BONG HITS 4 JESUS" at a school-sponsored event. School officials disciplined this student, and the student argued that their actions violated his rights to free speech. The clip can be found at http://www.youtube.com/watch?v=6x5hLOd-vUU.

paper copies

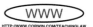

HTTP://WWW.CORWIN.COM/TEACHINGLAW

Table 2.1   Student Freedom of Expression Hypothetical Cases

Hypothetical Cases	Did Schools Violate Student Freedom of Expression?		
Case 1. Students in Yourtown Middle School were prohibited from wearing large buttons with a red slash through a swastika and the wording "NO SCHOOL UNIFORMS" to protest the new policy requiring all students to wear uniforms. Administrators felt that the buttons with the swastikas were offensive.	They Did	They Did Not	Don't Know
Case 2. In a high school journalism course that publishes the school newspaper, the teacher, Norm Nutral, prohibited any student editorial that endorses or criticizes any candidate running for the school board in order "to keep our schools out of local school politics."	They Did	They Did Not	Don't Know
Case 3. Each year, the student members of the high school drama club selected a popular Broadway musical for their annual show. But this year, the faculty advisor, Karol Kaution, rejected the student selection because it included profanity.	They Did	They Did Not	Don't Know
Case 4. A high school student, Calvin Cool, was suspended for refusing to take off a T-shirt that said "Legalize Pot." The principal explained that if Calvin was allowed to wear the shirt, other students or their parents might think the school was willing to tolerate an illegal activity.	They Did	They Did Not	Don't Know
Case 5. A student, Bob Anger, was suspended for two days because of his home Web site's "disrespectful" message to other students, saying that the school football coach was "lousy" and should be replaced.	They Did	They Did Not	Don't Know
Case 6. A teacher tells Henry Patrick that he may not be required to say the Pledge of Allegiance but that he must stand "in respectful silence." Henry is suspended when he refuses to stand.	They Did	They Did Not	Don't Know

(Continued)

(Continued)

Hypothetical Cases	Did Schools Violate Student Freedom of Expression?		
Case 7. A middle school student, Crit Jones, is prohibited from distributing her "underground" newspaper (that she printed at home) as classmates enter the school because it criticized the principal, superintendent, and school board for refusing to include a sex education course in the curriculum.	They Did	They Did Not	Don't Know
Case 8. Teacher Ron Respekt ordered a student to take off a "disrespectful" T-shirt that said, "President Obama is an International Terrorist." Mr. Respekt was concerned that the shirt might lead to conflict between students who supported the war in Iraq and those who opposed the war.	They Did	They Did Not	Don't Know
Case 9. Teacher I. M. Caring prohibited two student T-shirts that were designed to protest the high school's Tolerance Day. One shirt read, "Be Happy, Be Straight"; the other read, "Homosexuals are Sinful and Shameful."	They Did	They Did Not	Don't Know

Note: Principals can change the names and especially the grade levels when appropriate.

Rationale

Objectives

3 min

Rationale

It is important that teachers understand the law about student freedom of speech in order to respond effectively and legally when such issues arise.

Table 2.2   Controversial T-Shirt Examples

(Continued)

Table 2.2 (Continued)

Objectives

Post and/or state the following objectives for the lesson plan:

1. Teachers will be able to identify the constitutional principles established by the Supreme Court concerning the scope and limits of student freedom of expression in the public schools.

2. Teachers will be able to apply the reasoning of other federal and state decisions dealing with controversial student expression.

3. Teachers will be able to apply First Amendment principles and precedents to the kinds of student speech controversies that are likely to arise in the future.

The Law

12 min

Four U.S. Supreme Court decisions have given schools guidance about when they can and cannot restrict student speech. These cases include the principles for understanding the scope and limits of student freedom of speech.

POLITICAL SPEECH: *TINKER v. DES MOINES* (1969)

In 1965, students from Des Moines, Iowa, protested against the war in Vietnam by wearing black armbands to school. Since administrators had prohibited the armbands (fearing disruption), they suspended the protesters, who then took their case to court. In 1969, the U.S. Supreme Court ruled that *students do not "shed their constitutional right to freedom of speech or expression* at the schoolhouse gate (emphasis added)."

The Court explained that schools may not be "enclaves of totalitarianism," and fear of disturbance "is not enough to overcome the right to freedom of expression." As there was no evidence in this case that the armband wearers interfered with the school's work or the rights of other students, the Court ruled that the armbands were the kind of symbolic speech protected by the First Amendment.

The *Tinker* (1969) decision does not mean that schools cannot limit student expression. On the contrary, there are limits to all constitutional rights. Thus, the question in this and every case dealing with student expression is, When must schools tolerate and protect, or when can they prohibit and punish controversial speech? In *Tinker*, the Court ruled that schools cannot punish student speech because it is controversial or unpopular. However, schools can prohibit and discipline students if there is evidence that their speech "materially *disrupts class work* or involves *substantial disorder* or *invasion of the rights of others*" (emphasis added).

LEWD AND INDECENT SPEECH: *BETHEL SCHOOL DISTRICT v. FRASER* (1986)

This case arose when Matthew Fraser gave a nominating speech at a high school assembly that used an elaborate, graphic sexual metaphor to refer to his candidate. In this case, the Supreme Court ruled that the First Amendment does not protect student speech that is *"offensively lewd and indecent"* (emphasis added) in school-sponsored activities, even if it does not cause substantial disruption. Furthermore, the Court held that school officials have discretion to determine "what manner of speech" is vulgar and lewd in classrooms and school-sponsored activities.

SCHOOL-SPONSORED SPEECH: *HAZELWOOD SCHOOL DISTRICT v. KUHLMEIER* (1988)

In Hazelwood High School, the principal censored two stories from the school newspaper that was published by the Journalism II class. The principal deleted the stories to protect the privacy of the students and parents involved in the articles, and the Supreme Court ruled in his favor.

The Court explained that *educators can control* curriculum-related publications, school plays, and other *school-sponsored activities* that "bear the imprimatur" (i.e., official approval) of the school. This is because the school, as publisher of a newspaper or producer of a play, "may refuse to lend its name and resources" to student expression that does not meet its standards. In short, the Court ruled that educators do not violate the First Amendment by "exercising editorial control over the style and content of student speech in school-sponsored expressive activities so long as their actions are reasonably related to legitimate pedagogical concerns."

ADVOCATING ILLEGAL ACTIVITIES: *MORSE v. FREDERICK* (2007)

Joseph Frederick was suspended after displaying a banner that read "BONG HITS 4 JESUS" at a school-sponsored event on a street in front of his high school when the Olympic torch passed by. School administrators thought the banner encouraged drug use in violation of school policy. A majority of the Supreme Court agreed that the school could restrict Frederick's banner because *schools can prohibit student expression* that "they reasonably regard as *promoting illegal drug use*" (emphasis added). Some of the justices emphasized that this decision was consistent with *Tinker* (1969) and did not mean that schools could restrict student views just because they were offensive or were in conflict with the school's stated mission. Nor did *Morse* (2007) support any restriction on student speech "commenting on any political or social issue." Although *Morse* was a narrow decision that only applied to promoting illegal drug use, it is likely that it will allow schools to also restrict the direct promotion of other illegal activities.

In sum, these four decisions identified the scope and limits of student freedom of expression in public schools. In *Tinker* (1969), the Supreme Court ruled that the First Amendment does protect students' individual expression even if it is controversial, offensive, or unpopular. But, in *Tinker*, two limitations were recognized: speech that caused substantial disruption or speech that interfered with the rights of others. The three subsequent cases added three other limitations. *Bethel* (1986) excluded from First Amendment protection vulgar and lewd speech in school-related activities. *Hazelwood* (1988) excluded from protection curriculum and activities that were directly sponsored by and identified with the school. And *Morse* (2007) excluded student expression that promoted illegal activities.

Use presentation materials in Table 2.3 as handouts or slides to guide the discussion.

Table 2.3	Student Freedom of Expression Presentation Handouts or Slides

Slide 1: Political Speech

Tinker v. Des Moines (1969)
When must schools tolerate and protect and when can they prohibit or punish controversial speech?

Slide 2: Lewd and Indecent Speech

Bethel School District v. Fraser (1986)
Can schools prohibit vulgar and lewd speech if it doesn't cause a disruption?

Slide 3: School-Sponsored Speech

Hazelwood School District v. Kuhlmeier (1988)
When can schools control student newspapers or plays?

(Continued)

(Continued)

Slide 4: Advocating Illegal Activities

Morse v. Frederick (2007)
Can schools punish students who discuss illegal activity?

Alternative

Divide participants into four groups. Create handouts from the information provided for each case, and ask each group to answer one of the following questions:

1. When must schools tolerate and protect, and when can they prohibit or punish, controversial speech?
2. When can schools prohibit vulgar and lewd speech if it doesn't cause a disruption?
3. When can schools control student newspapers or plays?
4. Can schools punish students who discuss illegal activity?

Ask the groups to report out their answers to the larger group.

Application

Content to Practice

10 min

Assign teachers into three to nine groups depending on the number of participants. The teachers will return to discuss the 9 hypothetical cases that were previously considered. Each group will be provided 1 to 3 of the cases in Table 2.1 (see page 29). Instruct the groups to come up with a decision and rationale based on the content they received in the previous portion of the lesson. After each group has an opportunity to discuss their cases, distribute the responses from Table 2.4 (these can be individually cut out, or all the cases can be handed out). Each group will have an opportunity

(Text continued on page 39)

Table 2.4 Student Freedom of Expression Case Summaries

Case 1. *Violation.* Because this is a case of symbolic speech, the principles of *Tinker* (1969) apply. According to *Tinker,* students do not shed their constitutional rights to freedom of expression when they enter the public schools unless their expression causes substantial disruption or interferes with the rights of others. In this case, even if the buttons did offend some teachers and administrators, there was no evidence that they caused disruption or interfered with the rights of other students. Therefore, the students had a right to wear their buttons to protest the school's uniform policy, and the school's prohibition of their buttons was unconstitutional.

Case 2. *No violation.* This is a controversy about curriculum-related student expression. Therefore, the principles of the *Hazelwood* (1988) case apply. In contrast to *Tinker* (1969), which concerned individual student expression that happened to occur in school, Hazelwood concerned the school curriculum and held that educators have broad discretion to determine what is assigned in a course as long as their decisions have some educational purpose. In Case 2, the newspaper was published by the students as part of a Journalism course under the direction and supervision of teacher Norm Nutral, who had broad authority to decide what topics should and should not be discussed in the paper. Students (and even some teachers) might think it inappropriate or unwise to prohibit students from writing about local politics. But as long as Mr. Nutral has some legitimate reason for his decision, students have no constitutional right to challenge his judgment.

Case 3. *No violation.* Here, the principles of the *Bethel* (1986) and *Hazelwood* (1988) cases apply. In *Bethel,* the Court ruled that the First Amendment does not protect lewd and vulgar speech in a school-related activity even if it does not cause a disruption. Also, the Court allowed educators to decide what speech they consider vulgar or lewd. As the school play is a school-sponsored activity, the faculty advisor had the authority to reject the students' selection of a musical or play that included profanity, and therefore, Karol Kaution's decision did not violate the students' free-speech rights. In addition, applying the principles of *Hazelwood,* which give educators broad discretion to control school-sponsored, curriculum-related activities, would also lead a court to rule in favor of the school.

Case 4. *Violation.* This is a controversy where the principles of both *Tinker* (1969) and *Morse v. Frederick* (2007) apply. In *Morse,* the Court ruled that schools could prohibit and punish student speech that promoted illegal drug use. But, the Court also reaffirmed *Tinker's* protection for speech concerning social and/or political messages that did not cause disruption. If the T-shirt had said "Smoke Pot," school officials would have been able to require the student to take it off because it clearly promoted illegal drugs. But in this case, the message is clearly and primarily political and is not advocating any illegal activity. Therefore, the controversial T-shirt should be a protected form of student expression under the principles of *Tinker.*

(Continued)

(Continued)

Case 5. *Violation.* Here again, the *Tinker* (1969) decision applies. The First Amendment protects Bob Anger's messages that he disseminates to classmates using his home computer. This includes offensive and controversial views about teachers and coaches. Therefore, Bob should not be punished for criticizing school personnel as long as his messages were not defamatory and did not cause substantial disruption at school.

Case 6. *Violation.* Judges have ruled in favor of students who refuse to stand during the Pledge. Courts reason that schools cannot require students to engage in "implicit expression" by standing respectfully while the Pledge is being recited. As standing is an integral part of the Pledge ceremony, one judge wrote that, standing "can no more be required than the Pledge itself." Therefore, it was unconstitutional to require Henry Patrick to participate in that form of symbolic expression.

Case 7. *Violation.* An underground newspaper, like *Tinker's* (1969) armband, represents the views of an individual student, not the school. Therefore, students have the right to distribute their newspaper messages in school as long as the paper doesn't cause disruption and does not promote illegal activities. Schools can issue reasonable, content-neutral rules governing the time, place, and manner of the distribution. But, they cannot ban all distribution on campus before, during, or after school because they disagree with the paper's views. Therefore, Crit could not be prohibited from distributing her paper because of its criticism of the school's curricular decision.

Case 8. *Violation.* The *Tinker* (1969) decision is directly relevant to this case. Just as the principal in Des Moines couldn't prohibit Mary Beth Tinker from wearing her armband because of fear of disruption, so Mr. Respekt can't order the student to take off his anti-Bush T-shirt because of his concern that the shirt was "offensive" or "might" cause a conflict—unless he had evidence that would enable him to forecast substantial disruption.

Case 9. *Depends on the specific facts of the case.* The principles of *Tinker* (1969) apply to both T-shirts. But, it is likely that the shirt that said "Be Happy, Be Straight" would be protected if it did not cause disruption because it does not target any individual and is not a serious verbal attack against homosexual students. However, a prohibition of the "Homosexuals Are Sinful and Shameful" shirt could be upheld if the judge concluded that it collided with the rights of gay students to be secure and free from verbal assaults—especially where the school had a history of antigay conflicts. While *Tinker* principles apply to both T-shirts, the outcome in cases such as these may depend as much on the circumstances of the case as on the wording of the controversial messages.

---

to read the court ruling and perhaps modify their response before reporting out to the large group. The goal is to apply the principles and precedents of the Supreme Court and lower courts to determine whether the students' expressions would or would not be protected.

Assessment

5 min

To assess teachers' understanding, distribute four cards to each teacher (see Table 2.5). Ask them to fold the cards in half, review the summary of each case provided, and then to write their responses on the opposite side that relates to their current practice. You may need to ask teachers, "How might the knowledge of this case impact your practice?"

Table 2.5   Student Freedom of Expression Summary Cards

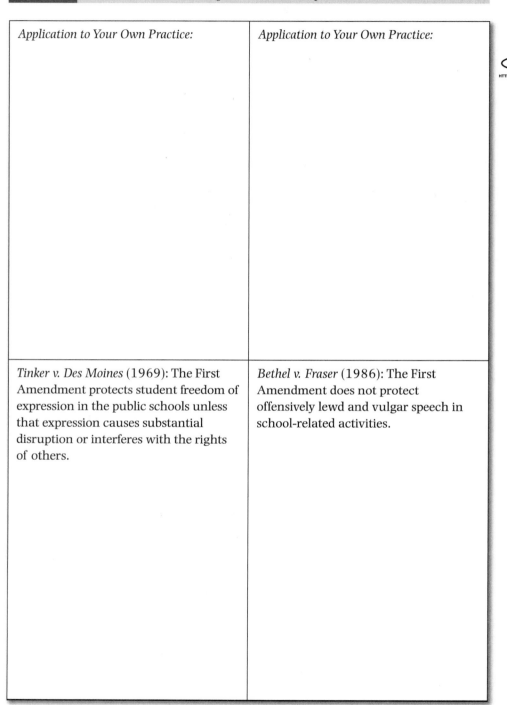

Application to Your Own Practice:	Application to Your Own Practice:
Tinker v. Des Moines (1969): The First Amendment protects student freedom of expression in the public schools unless that expression causes substantial disruption or interferes with the rights of others.	*Bethel v. Fraser* (1986): The First Amendment does not protect offensively lewd and vulgar speech in school-related activities.

paper copies

WWW
HTTP://WWW.CORWIN.COM/TEACHINGL

(Continued)

Table 2.5   Student Freedom of Expression Summary Cards

Application to Your Own Practice:	Application to Your Own Practice:
Morse v. Frederick (2007): Schools can punish student expression that promotes illegal activity.	*Hazelwood v. Kuhlmeier (1988).* Schools can control curriculum-related activities.

FAQ

10 min

As time permits, you may add some of these additional questions to the follow up discussion.

1. Does the First Amendment apply to elementary schools?

Probably. But, it might depend on the facts of the case.

In a recent 2007 decision, *DePinto v. Bayonne Board of Education* (2007), a federal court ruled in favor of elementary students who wore "No School Uniform" buttons. The judge rejected the school's argument that *Tinker* (1969) does not apply to elementary students. However, another judge wrote that "age is a critical factor in student speech cases," and the Supreme Court "has not suggested that fourth-graders have the same free expression rights of high school students." Thus, the answer might depend on both the age of the students and the nature of the speech in question.

2. Is a threat protected speech?

Not if it is a "true threat." Such a threat is unprotected if a reasonable person would interpret the statement as a serious expression of an intent to cause harm. Thus, a federal court upheld the expulsion of a junior high school student who wrote a letter describing how he would rape and murder a female classmate who broke up with him (*Doe v. Pulaski School District*, 2002). In contrast, a Michigan court ruled against the expulsion of a student who created "Satan's Web page" at home "for laughs" that included "people who are cool" and "people who I wish would die." After reviewing the facts of the case, the judge concluded that no reasonable person would think the statements on the Web site expressed a serious intent to harm anyone (*Mahaffey v. Aldrich*, 2002).

3. Can schools ban distribution of publications that promote religion?

No. Schools cannot restrict the distribution of materials by students because of the subject. Thus, an appeals court ruled against the policy of a school district in Illinois that banned distribution of all religious material in elementary and junior high schools because students might believe it was endorsed by the school. Instead of censorship, the judge suggested that educators teach students that schools do not endorse speech by permitting it and about why we tolerate divergent views (*Hedge v. Wauconda School District*, 1993).

4. **Can schools restrict the use of school computers?**

Yes. Schools have broad discretion to impose any reasonable regulations they wish on the use of school computers. For example, they can develop policies to prohibit inappropriate uses, such as violation of copyright laws, harassment of students or staff, commercial purposes, or the search for pornographic material. Or, they can simply restrict their use for specific academic purposes.

5. **Can schools restrict cell phones?**

Yes. Schools have authority to prohibit cell phone use that causes disruption or interferes with the rights of others. Or, schools can probably prohibit all cell phones in school. Although there are not yet any reported court decisions on this issue, schools probably have broad discretion to ban cell phones or restrict their use.

6. **Does the First Amendment apply to private or parochial schools?**

No. The First Amendment only applies to public schools. Its purpose is to prevent the government or government employees from restricting freedom of expression. Thus, students in nonpublic schools have no First Amendment rights.

7. **Does the student handbook give schools additional rights to restrict "inappropriate" speech?**

Not usually. If a school's rule states that teachers can censor student speech that they feel is "inappropriate" but does not cause substantial disruption or interfere with the rights of others, that rule is probably unconstitutional. School rules cannot contradict the constitution.

Resource Material

Related Cases

Over the years, a variety of state and federal courts have applied the principles and precedents of the Supreme Court to other student speech controversies. Instructors might want to mention some of these rulings:

- In Pennsylvania, a court upheld the expulsion of a middle school student who posted a Web site at home that harassed and threatened his algebra teacher and had a profoundly disruptive effect (*J. S. v. Bethlehem Area School District*, 2002).
- In Missouri, a high school student was suspended for creating a home Web page that used vulgar language and was critical of teachers and administrators. Applying the *Tinker* (1969) test, the court ruled in favor of the student because the Web page caused no disruption (*Beussink v. Woodland R-IV School District*, 1998).
- In a racially tense Kansas school, administrators prohibited student display of symbols or signs of racial conflict, such as black power or Confederate flags. A federal court upheld the restrictions because in a place of racial tension, a school does not have to wait for disruption to occur before taking action. In that situation, schools can restrict student expression when there is "a reasonable basis for forecasting disruption" (*West v. Derby Unified School District No. 260*, 2000).
- In New Jersey, a court ruled against an "overbroad" school code that prohibited speech that "creates ill will" because the code also prohibits "a significant amount of constitutionally protected speech." The fact that an expression causes hurt feelings, explained the court, does not mean that it is unprotected (*Sypniewski v. Warren Hills Regional Board of Education*, 2003).
- In Missouri, a court upheld the right of administrators to prohibit the marching band from playing a song that appeared to advocate drug use. Applying the principles of *Hazelwood* (1988), the judge ruled that prohibiting the school band from playing a song that advocated drug use was related to reasonable educational concerns (*McCann v. Fort Zumwalt School District*, 1999).
- In an Illinois case, a court upheld the right of a student to write a critical editorial in an underground paper (that was not sponsored by the school). Even though the editorial reflected a "disrespectful and tasteless attitude toward authority," that fact did not justify suspending the student for speech that did not cause substantial disruption (*Scoville v. Board of Education of Joliet Township*, 1970).
- A federal appeals court ruled against a student who wore a T-shirt that said "Homosexuality Is Shameful" on one side and "Be Ashamed, Our School Has Embraced What God Has Condemned" on the other. In this case, the school had a history of antihomosexual comments that had caused a series of altercations on campus. Furthermore, the court explained that the *Tinker* (1969) ruling not only excludes disruptive speech from First Amendment protection but also allows schools to restrict speech that "collides with the rights of other students to be secure and to be left alone." According to the court, this means that

students have the right to be free from psychological attacks and verbal assaults on their core identities—especially when they are members of minority groups that historically have been subject to verbal attack. (*Harper v. Poway Unified School District*, 2006).

Relevant Quotes

That [school boards] are educating the young for citizenship is reason for scrupulous protection of Constitutional freedoms of the individual, if we are not to strangle the free mind at its source and teach youth to discount important principles of our government as mere platitudes.

—West Virginia v. Barnette (1943)

Any word spoken in class, in the lunchroom or on the campus that deviates from the views of another person may start an argument or cause a disturbance. But our Constitution says we must take this risk: and our history says that it is this sort of hazardous freedom—this kind of openness—that is the basis of our national strength.

Students in schools as well as out of school are possessed of fundamental rights which the State must respect, just as they themselves must respect their obligations to the State. In our system, students may not be regarded as closed-circuit recipients of only that which the State chooses to communicate.

—Tinker v. Des Moines Independent School District (1969)

The undoubted freedom to advocate unpopular and controversial views in schools and classrooms must be balanced against the society's countervailing interest in teaching students the boundaries of socially appropriate behavior.

Surely it is a highly appropriate function of public school education to prohibit the use of vulgar and offensive terms in public discourse. . . . Vulgar speech and lewd conduct is wholly inconsistent with the "fundamental values" of public school education.

—Bethel School District v. Fraser (1986)

A school may, in its capacity as publisher of a school newspaper or producer of a school play disassociate itself . . . from speech that is, for example, ungrammatical, poorly written, inadequately researched, biased or prejudiced, vulgar or profane or unsuitable for immature audiences. . . . In addition, a school must be able to take into account the emotional maturity of the intended audience in determining whether to disseminate student speech on potentially sensitive topics.

—Hazelwood School District v. Kuhlmeier (1988)

Tinker warned that schools may not prohibit student speech because of a mere desire to avoid . . . an unpopular viewpoint. The danger here is far more serious and . . . extends well beyond an abstract desire to avoid controversy. . . . It was reasonably viewed as promoting illegal drug use.

—Morse v. Frederick (2007)

Supplies and Materials

In order to show the YouTube clip, the instructor will need access to the Internet during the lesson, or the YouTube clip can be converted to a number of formats that work off-line. One such conversion service can be found at http://www.zamzar.com. The clip can be converted to many formats. Most computers use MOV or MP4 files. If you use an MP3 format, only an audio file will be converted.

References

Bethel School District No. 403 v. Fraser, 487 U.S. 675 (1986).
Beussink v. Woodland R-IV School District, 30 F.Supp.2d 1175 (1998).
DePinto v. Bayonne Board of Education, 514 F.Supp.2d 633 (2007).
Doe v. Pulaski School District, 306 F.3d 616 (2002).
Harper v. Poway Unified School District, 445 F.3d 1166 (2006).
Hazelwood School District v. Kuhlmeier, 484 U.S. 260 (1988).
Hedge v. Wauconda School District, 9 F.3d 1295 (1993).
J. S. v. Bethlehem Area School District, 757A.2d 412 (2002).
Mahaffey v. Aldrich, 236 F.Supp.2d 779 (2002).
McCann v. Fort Zumwalt School District, 50 F.Supp.2d 918 (1999).
Morse v. Frederick, 551 U.S. 393 (2007).
Scoville v. Board of Education of Joliet Township, 425 F.2d 10 (1970).
Sypniewski v. Warren Hills Regional Board of Education, 307 F.3d 243 (2003).
Tinker v. Des Moines Independent School District, 393 U.S. 503 (1969).
West Virginia v. Barnette, 319 U.S. 624 (1943).
West v. Derby Unified School District No. 260, 206 F.3d 1358 (2000).

Additional Resources

Alexander, K., & Alexander, M. D. (2009). *American public school law* (7th ed.). Belmont, CA: Wordsworth. (SEE Chapter 8)
Fischer, L., Schimmel, D., & Stellman, L. (2010). *Teachers and the law* (8th ed.). Boston: Allyn and Bacon. (SEE Chapter 10)
Thomas, S., Cambron-McCabe, N., & McCarthy, M. (2009). *Public school law: Teachers' and students' rights* (6th ed.). Boston: Allyn and Bacon. (SEE Chapter 4)
Underwood, J., & Webb, L. D. (2006). *School law for teachers.* Upper Saddle River, NJ: Pearson. (SEE Chapter 7)

Special Education   3

BACKGROUND ON THE ISSUE

Historically, students with disabilities have experienced widespread exclusion. The students were often educated in separate schools and classrooms. As a result, laws have been passed by Congress to protect individuals with disabilities from discrimination. In 1975, the Education for All Handicapped Children's Act created special educational rights for students with disabilities. This law is now known as the Individuals with Disabilities Education Act (IDEA, 2004). In addition to this comprehensive law, Section 504 of the Rehabilitation Act of 1973 (Section 504, 2000), and the Americans with Disabilities Act (ADA; 1990) provide important legal protections for students with disabilities.

Teachers and school administrators consistently rank special education law as a topic that must be understood when working in a public school. These findings are not surprising, as teachers often confront legal issues when working with students with special needs. Thus, an understanding of these laws will help teachers better provide for students with disabilities in their classrooms and protect themselves from possible litigation.

Activator

Motivator

8 min

The principal will ask for four volunteers and will assign each teacher volunteer a role. (Note: The principal may want to identify and prepare the four teachers prior to this activity) The teachers will participate in a mock IEP meeting while reading from a prepared script. Before beginning the mock IEP meeting, the principal should read the background to set the context.

Background

Fred is autistic. His mother has been advocating support services in school. She recently came across applied behavior analysis (ABA) and believes that Fred's school should adopt this system. The following took place at an IEP meeting that was convened to discuss Fred's goals for the upcoming academic year.

Script

Special Education Teacher:	Thank you for coming to this IEP meeting to discuss Fred's goals. Based on Fred's most recent evaluation, we have decided to continue to provide Fred with support in his classes as well as some pullout support.
Parent:	Have you all heard about ABA?
Classroom Teacher:	No, what is that?
Principal:	Perhaps we should continue with our discussion about Fred's goals.
Parent:	(*Ignoring the principal*) ABA is a process called applied behavior analysis. I found an organization online that provides training and support for schools. They say it works very well with students like Fred because it helps decrease behavioral problems.
Special Education Teacher:	I have heard of it, but it was not part of our professional development this past year or this coming summer.
Parent:	I'd like Fred to be in a program like this.
Classroom Teacher:	Well, I think it's a good idea, but to start a new program at this time of the year could compromise my ability to provide for all children in my classroom. I'm worried that I just won't have the time to do ABA "right" and meet everyone else's needs.

paper copies

WWW
HTTP://WWW.CORWIN.COM/TEACHIN

Principal:	Our district doesn't have the human resources to sponsor individual therapy for students. I have complete confidence in our faculty and the program we provide to all our students in special education.
Occupational Therapist:	There is not conclusive evidence that ABA works with children. If this program isn't "research based," we shouldn't be using it.

After the meeting, Fred's mom said to the special education teacher, "I don't know, I am confused. If this is something that would help Fred, why won't the school get the program? What can I do if I think Fred is not getting the programming he needs?"

Ask the participants what they think about the IEP meeting. Guiding questions may include

- What were the legal issues that arose during the meeting?
- Does the parent have the right to appeal the decision not to use ABA?
- Does the school need to provide ABA if the program meets Fred's needs?

Rationale

Objectives

Rationale

3 min

There are more than 6 million students with disabilities in U.S. public schools. Lawsuits involving students with disabilities against school districts have been on the rise. With a greater understanding of the law, teachers will be able to avoid unnecessary lawsuits and better provide for their students.

Objectives

Post and/or state the following objectives for the lesson plan:

1. Teachers will be able to identify the key distinctions between IDEA, Section 504, and the ADA.

2. Teachers will be able to apply the laws to real-life classroom scenarios.

3. Teachers will be able to better confront special education issues arising in the classroom.

The Law

15 min

After reading the introductory background information below, the principal will divide teachers into three separate groups. Each group will be given markers and pieces of large butcher paper that stick to the wall. (If there are multiple groups on each topic, the principal may want to ask each group to share one important point to avoid redundancy. The principal will then go around to each group, asking for only one point at a time.)

- Group one will cover the Individuals with Disabilities Education Act (IDEA) (not including discipline).
- Group two will cover disciplining students with disabilities.
- Group three will cover Section 504 of the Rehabilitation Act and the Americans with Disabilities Act (ADA).

Each group will be provided with a content handout (see following pages). On the butcher paper, the teachers will highlight the most important aspects of the laws. This part of the activity should take between 7 and 10 minutes. Next, the teachers will present this information to the entire group, explaining and reviewing the key aspects of the law.

GROUP 1: INDIVIDUALS WITH DISABILITIES EDUCATION ACT

paper copies

IDEA (2004) is a federal-funding law, and currently all states accept federal funding under IDEA. The Act covers students from ages 3 to 21. The most recent congressional authorization of IDEA occurred in 2004. To be eligible for services under IDEA, the student's disability should fall under one or more of the following categories: mental retardation, hearing impairments, speech or language impairment, visual impairment, serious emotional disturbance, orthopedic impairments, autism, traumatic brain injury, other health impairments, or specific learning disability.

This lesson plan will discuss the basic provisions that teachers should know regarding IDEA. These provisions have been divided into the following two categories: (1) identifying students with disabilities and (2) providing for students with disabilities.

Identifying Students With Disabilities

States have the duty to identify children ages 0 to 21 who are in need of services. This duty is known as *child find*. A parent, a state education agency, or a local education agency may request an evaluation of a child who is suspected of having a disability. School personnel must obtain parental permission before conducting an evaluation. If a parent refuses to give consent, school officials may begin due-process procedures (discussed below) in order to proceed with the evaluation. School officials may also request that the parents or guardians participate in mediation when trying to reach consensus about an evaluation. It is important to note that school officials do not need to take due-process measures or go to mediation if the parents refuse the evaluation.

The evaluations must be accurate in order to ensure the proper placement of the child. To this end, a variety of assessment tools and strategies should be used (e.g., classroom observation and several types of tests). If the parents disagree with the school's evaluation, they may seek an independent evaluation. If the parents opt for an independent evaluation, the school district does not need to accept the results, but they must be considered.

Providing for Students With Disabilities

Each state must provide a student receiving services under IDEA with a *free appropriate public education* (FAPE). The definition of *appropriate* has been at issue in several court cases. FAPE does not need to *maximize* a student's learning potential; instead, a FAPE must merely provide a "basic floor of opportunity" for the student. All students receiving services under IDEA are entitled to FAPE.

The *individualized education program* (IEP) outlines how a student will receive a FAPE. Specifically, based on the student's evaluation, an IEP team prepares the IEP document. The IEP is designed to meet the unique needs of the child and outlines the goals and objectives for the child. The IEP team includes the parents, one general education teacher, one district administrator, one special education teacher, others with expertise that are relevant to the student's needs, and in some cases the student. Students typically participate when they are able to understand and participate in the discussion. School officials must ensure parental participation in the IEP process. Part of this responsibility includes providing parents with notice of their rights under IDEA.

Students with disabilities must be educated in the *least restrictive environment*—in other words, with students who are not disabled—to the maximum extent appropriate. Students with disabilities may only be removed from an educational setting with their general education peers when the instruction in the general education courses cannot be achieved satisfactorily. Factors that are considered in determining the least restrictive environment include the educational benefits of placing children with disabilities in the general education classroom, the nonacademic benefits of such placements, the effect that the presence of students with disabilities would have on others in the classroom, and the costs associated with the placement.

School districts must also provide *related services* so that a child with a disability can benefit from special education services. For example, a school district should provide bussing services to a student if this service is necessary to deliver special education. Courts have found, however, that medical services are not considered related services (although nursing services, occupational therapy, and physical therapy are considered related services).

Students with disabilities may be required to pass competency exams with accommodations before receiving a high school diploma. *Accommodations* might include questions in Braille, enlarged answer sheets, additional time, having tests read to students, or sign-language responses. Before taking a competency exam, students should be given appropriate notice about the exam and the opportunity to learn the academic content. IDEA also requires that school officials provide *transition services* for students with disabilities (beginning at age 14) who are shifting from school to independent living, work, or postsecondary education. The transition plan should be individualized to meet each student's needs.

Another provision under IDEA is *due process for parents,* which ensures fairness of educational decisions. Due process occurs when a parent expresses complaints regarding the child's evaluation, identification, or placement. Some of the related procedural safeguards for parents include (1) notification in writing of the referral; (2) ability to grant or deny permission to evaluate the student; (3) notification of IEP meetings (and the right to be present); (4) participation in all decision making regarding the child, with the exception of informal conversations between school officials; (5) bringing an advocate to meetings; and (6) the right to review all of the child's records. If there is a disagreement between the parents and school officials, either side may initiate a due-process hearing. It is important to note that IDEA requires that mediation be available to all parties before a due-process hearing is conducted. During the mediation session, a neutral third-party assists parents and school officials to develop a solution. If the issue is not settled in mediation, parents can initiate a due-process hearing. Such a hearing involves an independent hearing officer who ultimately makes a decision based upon the evidence presented. If either party is dissatisfied, a complaint can be filed in court.

GROUP 2: DISCIPLINING STUDENTS WITH DISABILITIES

Disciplining students with disabilities often raises a lot of questions for teachers. Basically, students with disabilities are disciplined in the same manner as students without disabilities, if there is no connection between their misconduct and the disability. However, if a student with a disability is suspended for more than 10 total, cumulative days during the school year, the IEP team and other relevant parties must conduct a *manifestation determination* to decide whether the student's disability is related to the misconduct. If a relationship exists, the IEP team needs to conduct *functional behavioral assessments* (FBA) and implement *behavior intervention plans* (BIP) into the IEP if necessary. When conducting an FBA, the IEP team develops educational programming that is related to supporting the student's behavioral problems. The team creates a BIP based on the FBA. The BIP should implement several strategies that would prevent the behavior at issue from reoccurring. It is also important to note that when a student who is receiving services under IDEA is removed for more than 10 days, it is generally considered a change in placement and requires that the child receives a new IEP. During the time that the new IEP is created, students need to remain in their original placement. This is known as the *stay-put provision*.

If the student brings a weapon to school, possesses illegal drugs at school, or inflicts serious bodily harm on another person at school, school officials may forego a manifestation determination and remove a student with a disability to an *interim alternative educational setting* (IAES) for up to 45 school days. In these cases, a student may be placed unilaterally in an IAES without the consent of a parent.

Students who have not yet been identified as needing services under IDEA might also get legal protection when removed from the classroom for more than 10 days. Specifically, if school officials knew or should have known that a student had a disability before the incident occurred, the student should not be removed until an IEP team determines the student's eligibility for special education services.

GROUP 3: SECTION 504 OF THE REHABILITATION ACT AND AMERICANS WITH DISABILITIES ACT

Unlike IDEA, Section 504 is a civil-rights law that prohibits those institutions receiving federal funds from discriminating against people with disabilities. Section 504 is a much broader law than IDEA and therefore protects more students. Students who are identified under IDEA also receive protections under Section 504. However, those students receiving services under Section 504 do not automatically receive services under IDEA (e.g., a student in a wheelchair may qualify under Section 504, but not IDEA).

To qualify for services under Section 504, the individual must be a person who has a physical or mental impairment that substantially limits one or more major life activity, has a record of such impairment, and is regarded as having such impairment. A major life activity may include but is not limited to seeing, hearing, walking, and talking. Individuals who qualify for services under Section 504 are entitled to reasonable accommodations to facilitate their participation in educational activities. Courts have found that an otherwise qualified individual, under Section 504, is someone who can meet all education or job requirements with reasonable accommodations. A *reasonable accommodation* might be Braille, a note taker, a sign-language interpreter, or more time on an assignment. On the other hand, a school would not be forced to allow a student who is legally blind to try out for the varsity basketball team—this would be an example of an unreasonable accommodation.

Similar to IDEA, students receiving services under Section 504 must be provided a free, appropriate public education and must be educated in the least restrictive environment. When determining FAPE, Section 504 compares the services and treatment provided to students with disabilities to those provided to students without disabilities. Students who qualify for services under this law are usually give a *504 accommodation plan*.

Similar to Section 504, the Americans With Disabilities Act (ADA, 2008) was designed to eliminate discrimination based on disability. Specifically, this law protects those individuals who have a physical or mental impairment that substantially limits one or more major life activities, have a record of impairment, or are regarded as having such impairment. The ADA incorporates all of the Section 504 law and expands its reach to include all entities—public or private. Both Section 504 and ADA apply to persons of all ages. Those students who are "otherwise qualified" must be permitted to participate in an educational program unless their participation poses a significant safety risk or an undue burden for the school district. In 2008, the ADA was amended. As a result, it is now easier for individuals seeking protection under the ADA to establish that they have a disability within the meaning of the ADA. Although the ADA is very similar to Section 504 for students, there is one major difference: The ADA requires that school districts *provide access* to individuals with disabilities who are attending school events. Thus, the ADA requires that athletic stadiums, lecture halls, and other facilities be barrier free (e.g., the school should ensure facilities have wheelchair ramps). When removing structural barriers from existing facilities, it must be "readily achievable" and not unduly expensive. When making new structures, however, the building must comply with ADA regulations and be barrier free.

After each group has the opportunity to create a set of notes on the butcher paper, distribute a note sheet provided below. Note: Also consider asking one person to take notes for the entire group. These notes can be distributed at a later time.

WHAT'S IMPORTANT TO KNOW ABOUT

paper copies

1. Individuals with Disabilities Education Act (IDEA):

2. Disciplining Students with Disabilities

3. Section 504 of the Rehabilitation Act and Americans with Disabilities Act

(Alternative)

Consider sending out the content to this lesson prior to the meeting. Along with the content, provide teachers with one of the three content areas to take notes on. This is one strategy to save time rather than having teachers reading during the professional development session.

Application

Content to Practice

14 min

After the butcher-paper presentations are complete, the principal will ask one teacher in each group to act as a moderator as the groups discuss each scenario below. Provide the moderator with the scenarios and guiding questions provided in Table 3.1. Table 3.2 is for the moderators' use.

Table 3.1	Special Education Scenarios

Scenario 1

Parents of an elementary school student with autism requested that the school district provide their child with the applied behavior analysis (ABA) method. The ABA method attempts to ensure a match between the behavioral intervention and the specific behavioral problems at issue. The ABA method is a comprehensive intervention to behavioral issues—it is ideally carried out in every setting possible.

The parents argued that their child would educationally benefit from the ABA method, and in making this argument, the parents cited several studies that demonstrated the effectiveness of ABA. The school district denied this request, arguing that it was too costly and that other methods were equally as effective.

Questions

1. Would the school district be denying this student FAPE if it did not implement the ABA method?
2. What if the parents pulled their child out of this school and sent him or her to a private school that used the ABA method? Would the parents be able to be reimbursed for the private-school tuition?
3. How would the parents appeal the school district's decision under IDEA?
4. How is it determined whether the ABA method is required under IDEA?

Scenario 2

A student receiving services under IDEA spray painted graffiti inside the school's restroom. The student painted "death to principal Stuckey." The student had already been suspended nine days this academic year. Thus, school officials needed to conduct a manifestation determination before suspending this student for five additional days. The parents argued that their child's diagnosis of ADHD was related to his misconduct; thus, he could not be suspended. (Note: Although ADHD is not listed as one of the 13 specific categories of disability, it is sometimes included under the "other health impairment" category.)

Questions

1. Do you think a diagnosis of ADHD could be found to be related to the conduct described above?

2. Do you think that school officials could have moved this student to an interim alternative educational setting for 45 days because of the "death threat" to principal Stuckey?

3. Would a manifestation determination need to be conducted before placing this child in an interim alternative-education setting? How would this be decided?

Scenario 3

A kindergarten student was diagnosed with acquired immunodeficiency syndrome (AIDS) from a contaminated blood transfusion received at birth. The child's doctors wrote the school district, indicating that there was no medical reason why the child should not be able to attend kindergarten. The school district allowed the child to attend kindergarten. After the child bit another classmate (no skin was broken), school officials had the child evaluated and decided that he should be tutored at home. The child's parents filed a lawsuit, contending that their son should be placed in the kindergarten classroom.

Questions

1. Would this child be found to be a "handicapped" person under Section 504? Is this student "otherwise qualified" to attend public school?

2. How do school officials balance the rights of the individual student and the safety of the rest of the students in the class?

Scenario 4

School officials dismissed a fifth-grade teacher who suffered epileptic seizures. The school district found out about the seizures because parents had seen the teacher have an episode at the mall and voiced concerns about student safety to the superintendent. After an investigation, school officials learned that even when the teacher took her medication, there was still a very small chance that she could have a seizure. The teacher suffered from approximately two seizures per year. The school board did not renew the teacher's contract. The teacher filed a lawsuit contending that the school board violated her rights under the Americans with Disabilities Act.

Questions

1. Is this teacher otherwise qualified?

2. What would this teacher argue under Section 504?

Table 3.2   Scenarios: Answers for Moderator

paper copies

Scenario 1

Question 1: It depends on the facts of the case. The school must provide an educational program that is considered "appropriate." An appropriate education is not necessarily the "best" education. Therefore, if the school's alternative is appropriate, then rejecting the parents' option does not deny FAPE. However, cost is never a justification to deny appropriate services. Further, even if what the parents are suggesting is better than the "floor of opportunity," school officials may want to provide the better services. In the long run, compromise is often less costly than due process and fosters a cooperative relationship.

Question 2: The parents would need to demonstrate that the child's placement in the public school was inappropriate and that the private school is appropriate (see *School Committee of Burlington v. Department of Education of Massachusetts*, 1985). Parents who unilaterally place their child in a private school are certainly taking a financial risk. If the public school placement was found to be appropriate, the parents would not be reimbursed.

Question 3: The parents must exhaust their administrative options under the IDEA first. Thus, the parents would first participate in a mediation and may eventually participate in a due-process hearing with an independent hearing officer.

Question 4: The IEP team would determine whether the ABA method provided the student with a FAPE.

Scenario 2

Question 1: We obviously need more facts about the student in this scenario, but this issue has certainly arisen in public schools before (see *Richland School District* v. *Thomas P.*, 2000). Based on the limited facts, however, it could be argued that the student's disability (ADHD) is related to the student's conduct (spray painting). Of course, it could be easily argued that there is no relation between the conduct and the disability. The IEP team would resolve this issue by analyzing the student's prior history and current diagnosis to determine if any relation exists.

Question 2: No. The student could only be unilaterally placed in an interim alternative educational setting for 45 days if the student inflicted another person with serious bodily harm. The student could also be moved to an interim alternative educational setting if the parents agreed. Decisions about the interim alternative educational setting are made by the IEP team, although it may be ordered by a due-process-hearing officer as well.

Question 3: In this case, the graffiti would not meet the three factors to justify an interim alternative educational setting (IAES) without a manifestation determination. However, the 45-day IAES may be used even when the conduct may be related to a student's disability. Thus, no manifestation determination is needed before placing the student in the interim alternative educational setting if drugs, weapons, or an assault was involved.

Scenario 3

Question 1: At least one court has found that the student was a "handicapped person" under Section 504 and was "otherwise qualified" to attend kindergarten in a public school setting after having been diagnosed with AIDS. The court reasoned that there was no significant evidence that the child posed any significant risk of harm to his classmates.

Question 2: In balancing this student's rights under Section 504 and the safety of his classmates, the court noted that there is no medical evidence that AIDS can be spread through biting (see *Thomas v. Atascadero Unified School District*, 1987; *District 27 Community School Board v. Board of Education of the City of New York*, 1986).

Scenario 4

Question 1: This teacher could reasonably argue that she was otherwise qualified under the ADA. In so doing, she might demonstrate that school officials could reasonably accommodate her by training several school officials about how to respond if a seizure were to occur in the classroom. For example, the school nurse or a teacher's aide could be trained in working with the teacher if a seizure occurred in the future.

Question 2: This teacher could also rely upon Section 504, arguing that although she has a physical impairment that substantially limits a major life activity, she is otherwise qualified to teach with reasonable accommodations. She would also contend that she has the necessary physical qualifications for the job.

Assessment

10 min

The principal will assess the participants using a strategy called "Stars and Wishes." The principal will hand out 3" × 5" cards and ask teachers to write three things learned on one side and three things they want to know more about on the other. After a few minutes, participants should be asked to share some of their responses to both questions. Principals need to consider what they do with the "wishes" list. For example, principals can provide a summary of the wishes to the district's special education director who might e-mail answers to the participants.

As time permits, you may add some of these additional questions to the follow-up discussion.

FAQ

10 min

1. **Are the suspension days for students receiving services under IDEA counted cumulatively or consecutively?**

   The regulations suggest that 10 cumulative days would be considered a change of placement. It is also important to note that after 10 cumulative days of suspension, educational services would need to be provided to the child. Also, when there is a request for a hearing, the stay-put provision applies, and the child will remain in his or her present educational placement unless school officials and parents agree on the child's placement.

2. **Must educational services be provided to students receiving services under IDEA if the suspension is 10 days or less?**

   No. When suspensions are less than 10 days, students are treated the same as general education students. If the suspension is more than 10 days, educational services must be provided.

3. **When must the IEP team convene to develop a behavioral intervention plan, if one has not already been completed?**

   Within 10 business days of any suspension that exceeds 10 cumulative days throughout the school year.

4. **Must school officials administer prescription medication to a student?**

   Yes. School officials must provide related services. This related service of administering medication is more akin to a service provided by a nurse rather than a doctor. Thus, school officials are required to administer medication to students.

5. **Could school officials require students with disabilities to take high-stakes tests?**

   Yes. If the student has been given adequate notice, appropriate curriculum, and necessary accommodations, a test may be administered. The student's IEP must describe the modifications to be made to enable students to participate in the testing. In several states, students with disabilities who do not pass the high-stakes testing requirements are still granted certificates of completion.

6. **What if the costs associated with the child's placement are considered too expensive by the school district?**

   The school must provide the most appropriate placement for the child without regard to the cost. However, it is important to note that *appropriate* does not mean that school officials are required to maximize a student's potential.

7. **If a parent requests year-round schooling for a student receiving services under IDEA, must the school district provide it?**

   Summer school services need only be provided if it is demonstrated that it provides the student with a FAPE. For example, if no services during the summer led to substantial regression, the school district must provide services.

8. **What law would teachers with disabilities rely upon?**

   Section 504 and the ADA would provide protections. In addition, states may have adopted laws providing protections for employees as well. For example, a high school teacher with a mobility impairment should be employed if a reasonable accommodation can be made to enable performance of essential functions.

9. **Are there state laws that impact students with disabilities?**

   Yes. States have enacted laws that oftentimes mirror and expand upon the requirements of IDEA.

10. **Can you expel a student in special education?**

    Yes. If the student's conduct is not related to his or her disability, the student can be expelled. However, during the expulsion, the student must receive educational services as provided by the IEP until age 21. Thus, students in special education cannot be expelled in the same manner as non–special education students (because the school district must continue educational services to the student in special education).

11. **Can parents request that their children be removed from special education programs?**

    Yes. Parents can revoke consent for placement and remove their children from special education at any time without mediation or due process.

12. **Must charter schools accept students with disabilities?**

    Yes. Charter schools must follow federal and state laws. As such, charter schools may not exclude students with disabilities.

13. Who is really responsible for implementing the IEP?

Everyone on the IEP team. However, the classroom teachers *must* ensure that it is implemented on a daily basis.

Resource Material

Relevant Quotes

We know that education is the key to our children's future, and it is the IDEA that ensures all children with disabilities have access to a free appropriate public education. We have seen tremendous progress over the past 25 years—students with disabilities are graduating from high school, completing college, and entering the competitive workforce in record numbers—and we must continue this progress over the next 25 years and beyond.

—President Bill Clinton (2000, in Katsiyannis, Yell, & Bradley, 2001, p. 324)

Free appropriate public education . . . evinces a congressional intent to bring previously excluded handicapped children into the public education systems of the states and to require the states to adopt procedures which would result in individualized consideration of and instruction for each child.

—Board of Education v. Rowley (1982)

A basic floor of opportunity provided by the Act [IDEA] consists of access to specialized instruction and related services which are individually designed to provide educational benefit to the handicapped child.

—Board of Education v. Rowley (1982)

Supplies and Materials

- Butcher paper and markers
- 3" × 5" cards

References

American with Disabilities Act of 1990, 42 U.S.C. sec. 12101 (1990) (as amended 2008).

Board of Education of the Hendrick Hudson Central School District v. Rowley, 458 U.S. 176 (1982).

District 27 Community School Board v. Board of Education of the City of New York, 502 N.Y.S.2d 325 (N.Y. 1986).

Individuals with Disabilities Education Improvement Act, 20 U.S.C. sec. 1400 (2004).

Richland School District v. Thomas P., 2000 U.S. Dist. Lexis 15162 (Wis. 2000).

School Committee of Burlington v. Department of Education of Massachusetts, 471 U.S. 359 (1985).

Section 504 of the Rehabilitation Act of 1973, 29 U.S.C. sec. 794 (2000).

Thomas v. Atascadero Unified School District, 662 F.Supp. 376 (Cal. 1987).

Additional Resources

Alexander, K., & Alexander, M. D. (2009). *American public school law* (7th ed.). Belmont, CA: Wadsworth. (SEE Chapter 10)

Fischer, L., Schimmel, D., & Stellman, L. (2010). *Teachers and the law* (8th ed.). Boston: Allyn and Bacon. (SEE Chapter 17)

Katsiyannis, A., Yell, M., & Bradley, R. (2001). Reflections on the 25th anniversary of the Individuals with Disabilities Education Act. *Remedial and Special Education, 22,* 324–334.

LaMorte, M. (2008). *School law: Cases and concepts.* Boston: Pearson Education. (SEE Chapter 6)

Russo, C. (2004). *Reutter's the law of public education* (5th ed.). New York: Foundation Press. (SEE Chapter 14)

Thomas, S., Cambron-McCabe, N., & McCarthy, M. (2009). *Public school law: Teachers' and students' rights* (6th ed.). Boston: Allyn and Bacon. (SEE Chapter 6)

Underwood, J., & Webb, L. D. (2006). *School Law for Teachers.* Upper Saddle River, NJ: Pearson. (SEE Chapter 8)

Yell, M. (2006). *The law and special education.* Upper Saddle River, NJ: Pearson Prentice Hall.

Discipline 4

*Student Due Process
and Search and Seizure*

BACKGROUND ON THE ISSUE

When most people think of due process, they think of courtroom trials portrayed on television—of lawyers, judges, juries, witnesses, and dramatic cross-examinations. When people think of search and seizure, they may think of the Fourth Amendment—of warrants, probable cause, and motions to suppress evidence that was seized illegally. The key question addressed in this lesson is: Do these constitutional protections apply to students in the public schools? Specifically,

- Are students entitled to due process? If so, what process is due?
- Does the Fourth Amendment protect students against unreasonable search and seizure?

Before the Supreme Court ruled on these questions, many educators feared that if the Bill of Rights applied to students, schools would become courtrooms and education would become an adversarial process. These fears, however, have proved to be greatly exaggerated. This is because the Court has applied the Constitution very differently to students in the public schools than to adults in their homes. This chapter explains and clarifies these differences.

Activator

Motivator

7 min

The principal should read each of the scenarios below one at a time. Ask teachers to respond to the set of questions after each scenario.

Scenario 1: Due Process

Al Anger walked into Principal Pal's office with a note from his teacher stating that Al started a fight in her classroom for the second time this month. Mr. Pal told Al that because of his fighting, he might be suspended. But before he suspended Al, Pal asked if Al had anything to say for himself. Al spent 10 minutes explaining that he didn't start the fight and that he was entitled to a due-process hearing that included an opportunity for his parents to question his teacher, to have some of his classmates testify on his behalf, and to have his family lawyer advise him. The principal told Al that he believed the teacher, that Al just had his hearing, and that he was being suspended for three days.

Ask teachers, by a show of hands, what they think about each of the statements in Table 4.1. You may want to tally the responses for the group. Ask teachers to hang on to the handout, as they will be returning to it later.

paper copies

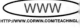

WWW
HTTP://WWW.CORWIN.COM/TEACHINGL

| **Table 4.1** | Due Process Scenarios |

Al's Issue			
1. Al has a right to some type of due-process hearing before being suspended for one to three days.	True	False	Unsure
2. Al has a right to bring a parent to a meeting with the principal before being suspended for more that three days.	True	False	Unsure
3. Before being suspended for five days, Al has a constitutional right to bring a lawyer to a hearing to advise him.	True	False	Unsure

Al's Issue			
4. Before suspending Al for 5 days, the principal must investigate Al's claim by talking with the teacher and/or some of the students.	True	False	Unsure
5. Before being expelled, Al has a right to a formal hearing that includes a written statement of the evidence against him, the right to bring witnesses on his behalf, to question witnesses against him, plus the right to appeal.	True	False	Unsure
6. If Al were a student in special education, he would have additional due-process rights.	True	False	Unsure

Scenario 2: Search and Seizure

Read each of the cases in Table 4.2, and ask teachers to indicate, by a show of hands, whether they agree, disagree, or are unsure about the claims of Bully's lawyer in Cases 1 and 2 and the claims of the parents in Case 3 and 4. Tally the responses in the right-hand column. Ask teachers to hang on to the handout, as they will be returning to it later.

Alternative

As an alternative activity, principals can discuss the contents of a YouTube clip about the car and locker searches in a school district. This clip discusses how school officials permitted suspicionless searches of students' cars and lockers. Show the clip at http://www.youtube.com/watch?v=gQbwyr6FGOg to the participants.

After showing the clip, the principal should lead the teachers through a three-to-five-minute discussion about whether it was okay to allow these suspicionless searches.

Case			
Case 1. A student at Yourtown High told Mr. Kalm, the eighth-grade teacher, that she saw Bully Barnes put a long knife in his backpack. Kalm asks Bully if he can look in his backpack for a knife. Bully says, "Sure, 'cause I don't have a knife." Kalm looks through the backpack and can't find a knife. But Kalm opens Bully's wallet and finds an envelope with a substance that he gives to the principal that turns out to be marijuana. The principal then turns the marijuana over to the police. At Bully's trial, his lawyer claims that the search of his backpack was illegal, and therefore, the marijuana can't be used as evidence against him.	Agree	Disagree	Unsure
Case 2. Suppose Mr. Kalm had been told that Bully had marijuana in an envelope in his backpack, and when Kalm searched Bully's backpack for the marijuana, he couldn't find any, but he did find a long knife. When a prosecutor introduces the knife as evidence in court, Bully's lawyer claims that the knife was seized illegally since there was no reason to believe Bully had a knife in his backpack.	Agree	Disagree	Unsure
Case 3. When a student tells principal Kal Koncern that Sharon Shy gave her a pain pill in violation of school rules, Kal tells the nurse to search Sharon. Finding no pills in Sharon's backpack or outer clothing, the nurse continues the search by telling Sharon to take off her clothes and pull out her bra and underwear. After no pills are found, Sharon's mother claims that the search violated Sharon's Fourth Amendment rights.	Agree	Disagree	Unsure
Case 4. The Yourtown school board is concerned about drug use. Therefore, the Board wants to require all students who want to participate in any extracurricular activity to sign a waiver agreeing to submit to random, suspicionless drug testing. Some parents claim that forcing their children to submit to drug testing when there is no reasonable suspicion that they have used drugs is a violation of their Fourth Amendment privacy rights.	Agree	Disagree	Unsure

Table 4.2 Search and Seizure Scenarios

HTTP://WWW.CORWIN.COM/TEACHING

paper copies

Rationale

Objectives

Rationale

3 min

Teachers often worry about what the legal limits are regarding school disciplinary issues within their classrooms. It is important that teachers understand this area of law in order to respond effectively and legally when such issues arise.

Objectives

Post and/or state the following objectives for the lesson plan:

1. Teachers will understand why and how the U.S. Supreme Court and other courts have applied the Due Process Clause to students in public schools in cases of suspension and expulsion.

2. Teachers will understand why and how the courts have applied the Fourth Amendment to students in public schools.

The Law

20 min

Two big ideas—*due process* and *search and seizure*—are the focus of the content below. In this activity, you will ask groups of teachers to conduct a vocabulary activity called a Frayer Diagram. Begin by explaining that a Frayer Diagram is a method employed to understand difficult terms. The process begins by providing an example of a Frayer Diagram structure. In Table 4.3, a term is placed in the center and each quadrant answers a specific question.

Divide teachers into eight groups, and assign each group one term and one Frayer Diagram from Tables 4.3 and 4.4. Also provide teachers with the notes on pages 74–76. After five to seven minutes, ask a representative from each group to report out on their diagrams. (You may want to collect the diagram cards, make copies for teachers, and distribute them.)

Table 4.3   Due Process Key Terms

The Law	Examples
Due Process	
Definition (your own words)	Implications for Teachers

The Law	Examples
Informal Notice and Hearing	
Definition (your own words)	Implications for Teachers

paper copies

WWW
HTTP://WWW.CORWIN.COM/TEACHIN

The Law	Examples

Formal Notice and Hearing	
Definition (your own words)	Implications for Teachers

The Law	Examples

Manifestation Determination	
Definition (your own words)	Implications for Teachers

paper copies

Table 4.4   Search and Seizure Key Terms and Cases

The Law	Examples
Reasonable Suspicion	
Definition (your own words)	Implications for Teachers

The Law	Examples
BOE v. Earls (2002)	
Definition (your own words)	Implications for Teachers

paper copies

WWW
HTTP://WWW.CORWIN.COM/TEACHING

The Law	Examples
New Jersey v. T.L.O. (1985)	
Definition (your own words)	Implications for Teachers

The Law	Examples
Safford Unified School District No. 1 v. Redding (2009)	
Definition (your own words)	Implications for Teachers

paper copies

NOTES FOR DISTRIBUTION

paper copies

Due Process

In *Goss v. Lopez* (1975), the U.S. Supreme Court ruled that students do not "shed their constitutional rights at the schoolhouse gate." Therefore, they are entitled to some form of due process if they are faced with a possible suspension for 1 to 10 days. This is because a suspension of up to 10 days is not so minor a punishment that it may be imposed "in complete disregard of the Due Process Clause."

Due process is a flexible concept. It varies according to the possible seriousness of the penalty: The more serious the possible penalty, the more formal the process that is due.

In cases of a short 1-to-10-day suspension, the process required is an informal notice and hearing. The *informal notice* may be oral or in writing and consists of telling students what they are accused of doing and what school rule they are charged with breaking. According to the Supreme Court, if they deny the charge, students are entitled to an *informal hearing* that consists of (1) "an explanation of the evidence the authorities have" and (2) "an opportunity to tell his side of the story" before the disciplinarian decides on what, if any, punishment to impose (*Goss v. Lopez*, 1975). The concern of the Court is that there be at least "rudimentary precautions against unfair or mistaken findings of misconduct" and arbitrary suspensions from school. Thus, the Court does not turn schools into courtrooms or require formal due process in cases of short-term suspensions. In fact, the informal process required in these cases is the minimum that most good disciplinarians would follow even if there were no court rulings about student suspensions.

In cases of long-term suspension or expulsion, a *formal notice* and *formal hearing* is required. Because such serious penalties can have serious consequences on a student's education and employment opportunities, meticulous procedures must be followed. These consist of a written notice that informs students and their parents of the charges, witnesses, and evidence against them and of their procedural protections at the hearing, including the right to question their accusers, to bring witnesses and evidence on their behalf, to have someone represent them, and to record the hearing and appeal the decision.

Additional procedures are required for students with special needs. Before they can be suspended for more than a total of 10 days during the school year, there must be a *manifestation determination*. This means that an individual educational program (IEP) team meeting must be called to determine whether the misbehavior is a manifestation of the student's disability. If not, the student can be disciplined like any other student. If the team concludes that the misbehavior is a manifestation of the disability, then standard discipline cannot take place, and the team must conduct a functional-behavioral assessment and develop a behavior intervention plan to address the behavior and/or modify the existing plan. (For more on disciplining students with special needs, see Chapter 3).

In sum, due process is not a fixed or inflexible concept that requires the same procedures in all discipline cases. Instead, it is a concept based on fairness that requires more formal procedures before more serious penalties are imposed. That is the reason judges require a formal notice and hearing before expelling a student, an informal process before a 1-to-10-day suspension, and no due process before minor punishments, such as detention or probation.

Copyright © 2010 by Corwin. Additional materials and resources related to *Principals Teaching the Law: 10 Legal Lessons Your Teachers Must Know* can be found at http://www.corwin.com/teachinglaw.

NOTES FOR DISTRIBUTION

paper copies

Search and Seizure

In *New Jersey v. T.L.O.* (1985), the Supreme Court ruled that the Fourth Amendment's protection against unreasonable *search and seizure* applies to students in the public schools. However, the Court explained that educators are not required to comply with the requirements that apply to police who must obtain a warrant from a judge based on probable cause before searching citizens in their homes. Educators do not need a warrant. Instead of *probable cause* (a relatively high standard of evidence required of police before a judge will issue a warrant), the lower standard required of teachers or administrators is *reasonable suspicion.* Specifically, to justify a search by educators, the search must be reasonable in its *inception* and in its *scope.* To be reasonable in inception, a school official must be able to articulate some objective reason for the search. Furthermore, the scope of the search must be related to its reason and not be excessively intrusive in light of the age and sex of the student and the nature of the infraction. For example, if one student reported that he saw another student put a pistol in his backpack, it would be reasonable in inception to search the backpack. But, it would not be reasonable in scope for the educator to open and search the wallet in the backpack because it could not contain a pistol.

In *Board of Education v. Earls* (2002), the Supreme Court held that schools could require students to sign waivers permitting random, suspicionless drug testing as a condition for participating in *any* extracurricular activity. In a five-to-four decision, the majority reasoned that participation in extracurricular activities is a privilege and not a right. The Court further justified its decision based on the school's responsibility to protect the health and safety of students and on its belief that the goal of a drug-free school outweighed the limited invasion of privacy involved in random urine testing.

In *Safford Unified School District No. 1 v. Redding* (2009), the Supreme Court ruled that information from one student that a classmate gave her a pain pill in violation of school rules constituted reasonable suspicion to justify a search of the student's backpack and outer clothing. But, the Court also ruled that proceeding to a strip search was not reasonable in scope because the search was for a common pain reliever that posed no danger to the students (based on the power of the drug or its quantity) and there was no reason to think the student was carrying pills in her underwear. Thus, a search, even if justified at its inception, crosses the constitutional boundary when it becomes excessively intrusive in light of the age and sex of the student—especially when the object of the search poses no danger to students.

Application

Content to Practice

15 min

Ask teachers to revisit the hypothetical cases from the start of this lesson. Individually or in small groups, ask teachers to answer the questions regarding due process in Table 4.5 and search and seizure in Table 4.6. The answers to each of the scenarios are provided below for the principal to share.

Table 4.5   Due Process Scenarios Revisited

Due Process		
Issue	**True/False**	**Why?**
1. Al is entitled to some type of due-process hearing before being suspended for one to three days.		
2. Al is entitled to bring a parent to a meeting with the principal before being suspended for more that three days?		
3. Before being suspended for more than five days, Al would be entitled to bring a lawyer to a hearing to advise him.		

paper copies

WWW

HTTP://WWW.CORWIN.COM/TEACHIN

Due Process		
Issue	**True/False**	**Why?**
4. Before suspending Al for more than five days, the principal must investigate Al's claim by talking with the teacher and/or some of the students.		
5. Before being expelled, Al would be entitled to a formal hearing that included a written statement of the evidence against him, the right to have someone represent him, to bring witnesses on his behalf, to question witnesses against him, plus the right to record the hearing and appeal the decision.		
6. If Al were a student in special education, he would have additional due-process rights.		

Table 4.6 Search and Seizure Scenarios Revisited

Search and Seizure		
Case	**Agree/ Disagree**	**Why?**
1. A student at Yourtown High told Mr. Kalm, the eighth-grade teacher, that she saw Bully Barnes put a long knife in his backpack. Kalm asks Bully if he can look in his backpack for a knife. Bully says, "Sure, 'cause I don't have a knife." Kalm looks through the backpack and can't		

(Continued)

(Continued)

Search and Seizure		
Case	Agree/ Disagree	Why?
find a knife. But Kalm opens Bully's wallet and finds an envelope with a substance that he gives to the principal and that turns out to be marijuana. The principal then turns the marijuana over to the police. At Bully's trial, his lawyer claims that the search of his backpack was illegal, and therefore the marijuana can't be used as evidence against him.		
2. Suppose Mr. Kalm had been told that Bully had marijuana in an envelope in his backpack; when Kalm searched Bully's backpack for the marijuana, he couldn't find any, but he did find a long knife. When a prosecutor introduces the knife as evidence in court, Bully's lawyer claims that the knife was seized illegally as there was no reason to believe Bully had a knife in his backpack.		
3. When a student tells principal Kal Koncern that Sharon Shy gave her a pain pill in violation of school rules, Kal tells the nurse to search Sharon. Finding no pills in Sharon's backpack or outer clothing, the nurse continues the search by telling Sharon to take off her		

Search and Seizure		
Case	Agree/ Disagree	Why?
clothes and pull out her bra and panties. After no pills are found, Sharon's mother claims that the search violated Sharon's Fourth Amendment rights.		
4. The Yourtown school board is concerned about drug use. Therefore, the board wants to require all students who want to participate in any extracurricular activity to sign a waiver agreeing to submit to random, suspicionless drug testing. Some parents claim that forcing their children to submit to drug testing when there is no reasonable suspicion that they have used drugs is a violation of their Fourth Amendment privacy rights.		

Due Process Answers

1. True

According to the Supreme Court decision in *Goss v. Lopez* (1975), Al Anger is entitled to an informal hearing before being suspended for 1 to 10 days. This consists of telling Al what rule he is accused of breaking. If he denies the accusation, he is entitled to know the evidence against him and to be given an opportunity to tell his side of the story before the principal decides on what, if any, punishment to impose.

2. False

Although some schools allow a student to bring a parent to a conference before imposing a suspension if the student is not a danger to himself or others, this is a matter of discretion and is not required by the courts.

3. False

Al does not have a constitutional right to bring a lawyer to advise him in the informal hearing that is required before a short-term suspension. According to the Supreme Court opinion in *Goss v. Lopez* (1975), "further formalizing the suspension process . . . may not only make it too costly as a regular disciplinary tool but also destroy its effectiveness as part of the teaching process." However, some courts have held that in an expulsion case, Al would have a right to bring a lawyer to attend the hearing and advise him because of the seriousness of the possible penalty.

4. False

The *Goss v. Lopez* (1975) decision does not always require the principal to investigate Al's story, but under some circumstances, that would be the appropriate thing to do.

5. True

Before an expulsion, Al would be entitled to a written notice that advised him of the charges and evidence against him and of his right to bring someone to represent him, witnesses and evidence on his behalf, as well as his right to question witnesses and his right to record the hearing and appeal the decision.

6. True

If Al were a student in special education, he could not be suspended for more than 10 days during a school year unless his IEP team held a manifestation determination that concluded that his misbehavior was not caused by his disability.

Search and Seizure Answers

1. Bully's lawyer is *right.*

The search of Bully's wallet and the seizure of his marijuana were illegal. According to the *New Jersey v. T.L.O.* (1985) decision, the Fourth Amendment requires that a search by educators must be reasonable in inception and scope. Based on what the student informant told Kalm, it was reasonable in inception for him to search the backpack for the long knife. But it was not reasonable in scope to search the wallet, as a long knife could not be in the wallet. Therefore, if a prosecutor wanted to introduce the drugs as evidence in a criminal trial, Bully's lawyer would probably be successful in having the evidence ruled inadmissible.

2. The *seizure* of the knife was *legal.*

    Based on the student informant's information, Kalm's search of the backpack to look for the drugs was reasonable in inception and scope. Because Kalm found the knife in plain view incidental to a search for drugs, the search was not excessive in scope. Therefore, the judge would allow the knife to be entered in evidence against Bully.

3. The strip search was *not legal.*

    Applying the principles of *Safford v. Redding* (2009) to the facts of this case, the search violated Sharon's Fourth Amendment rights. Although the initial search of Sharon's backpack and outer clothing was reasonable in inception, the search was not reasonable in scope because the pills posed no danger to students, and because there was no reason to believe Sharon was hiding them in her underwear.

4. The drug testing would be *legal.*

    According to the *Board of Education v. Earls* (2002) decision, public schools have discretion to require students who want to participate in extracurricular activities to sign waivers allowing school officials to engage in random, suspicionless drug testing. There is much debate about whether such a requirement is wise and cost-effective. But, it is now clear that such a policy does not violate the Fourth Amendment.

Assessment

5 min

At the beginning of the lesson, two questions were highlighted as the primary function of this lesson. Now, in the assessment, return to these two questions. Provide teachers with a ticket (see Figure 4.1) to leave the meeting. On one side, ask the teachers to answer the question: Are students entitled to due process? If so, what process is due? On the other, ask them to respond to the other question: When may educators search students without violating the Fourth Amendment?

Figure 4.1 Assessment Tickets

paper copies

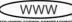

WWW
HTTP://WWW.CORWIN.COM/TEACHING

Alternative

Use the following true-false assessment:

1. Students are entitled to an informal notice and hearing before short suspensions of 1 to 10 days.

2. Before being expelled, students must be provided with a lawyer by the school if they can't afford one.

3. Administrators can strip search students if they have reasonable suspicion that the student stole large sums of money.

4. Before being expelled, students are entitled to a formal notice and hearing. The written notice must inform students and their parents of the evidence against them and of their rights at the hearing, including the opportunity to have someone represent them, to bring witnesses and evidence on their behalf, to question their accusers, to record the hearing, and to appeal.

5. Students have a right to remain silent when questioned by teachers about violations of school rules.

6. To justify a search of students' clothing, backpacks, or cars, teachers or administrators need "reasonable suspicion." To meet this standard, the search must be reasonable in its inception and reasonable in scope.

7. Schools may require students to sign waivers to permit random, suspicionless drug testing in order to participate in extracurricular activities.

1. **True**

2. **False** *(In many states, students may bring a lawyer to an expulsion hearing to advise them, but the school is not required to furnish a lawyer for the student.)*

3. **False** *(Strip searches are only permitted in situations that pose a serious danger to the student or others.)*

4. **True**

5. **False** *(This right only applies to criminal law.)*

6. **True**

7. **True**

FAQ

10 min

As time permits, you may add some of these additional questions to the follow-up discussion.

1. Do *Miranda* warnings apply to students?

No. In *Miranda v. Arizona*, 377 U.S. 201 (1966), the Supreme Court ruled that the Fifth Amendment privilege against self-incrimination applies in a criminal investigation and requires that suspects be informed of their right to remain silent, that what they say may be used against them, and that they have a right to have a lawyer represent them.

These rules do not apply to educators or to school-resource officers employed by the school who question students in public schools, as school discipline is not a criminal proceeding. However, *Miranda* (1966) would apply to police who question students in school as part of a criminal investigation.

2. Is due process required before in-school suspension?

Not usually. In a 2007 decision (*Laney v. Farley*, 2007), a federal appeals court ruled that a student was not entitled to notice and an opportunity to be heard before an in-school suspension. The court reasoned that an in-school suspension does not deprive a student of educational opportunities the way an out-of-school suspension does. However, the court recognized that under certain circumstances, in-school isolation might constitute as much deprivation of education as at-home suspension.

3. Must due process be used before corporal punishment?

Not in those states or school districts that permit corporal punishment. The Supreme Court has ruled that corporal punishment is not unconstitutional and that it is a matter for state legislatures and local school districts to decide whether to permit such punishment and, if so, what procedures to require (*Ingraham v. Wright*, 1977). However, courts have ruled that grossly excessive corporal punishment may be unconstitutional, and such punishment probably also violates state law.

4. Are strip searches unconstitutional?

Often, but not always. Strip-searching two second-grade students for a missing $7 dollars was ruled clearly unconstitutional (*Jenkins by Hall v. Talladega*, 1996). In that case, the court suggested a continuum: At one extreme are dangerous weapons and drugs that might justify a strip search. At the other extreme are small amounts of money, personal items, and "nondangerous" contraband that would never justify strip searches. Similarly, it is likely that a strip search for $50 missing from a teacher's purse would be considered unreasonable because the theft would involve little danger to others and thus could not justify a highly invasive search. In cases where school officials feel that students should be strip searched because of substantial evidence of criminal behavior, such as possession of dangerous weapons or distribution of illegal drugs, it might be wise to have police—rather than educators—conduct such searches.

5. What about searches of student lockers or cars?

Lawyers differ about whether the Fourth Amendment even applies to lockers. Most lawyers believe that students have no reasonable expectation of privacy in their lockers. This is because the lockers are owned by the school, and school rules usually make it clear that the lockers are subject to search by school officials—especially when they have the combination of the locks. Other lawyers believe that educators should have some individual suspicion before they search a student's locker—especially if they search jackets or other items owned by the student in the locker. This is based on the theory that students do not lose their reasonable expectation of privacy in their clothing when they put it in their locker.

Courts consider the search of a car on school property more like the search of a backpack than a locker, and the principles of *New Jersey v. T.L.O.* (1985) should apply. Thus, to comply with the

Fourth Amendment, educators' searches of students' cars should be based on individual suspicion and reasonable in inception and reasonable in scope.

6. Is it constitutional for administrators to use video cameras for surveillance?

Usually it is. Video cameras may be used in school hallways, cafeterias, libraries, parking lots, and other "common areas" without violating constitutional principles. However, the Fourth Amendment might be violated if video cameras were placed in school bathrooms, locker rooms, or private offices where people have a "reasonable expectation of privacy."

7. If students consent to a search, do they lose their Fourth Amendment protections?

Yes, if they consent *voluntarily.* In a school setting, however, a student's lawyer might raise two questions: Is it reasonable to hold that students waived their rights if they didn't know them? Second, was the student's acquiescence to an administrator's request to search really voluntary? The answers may depend on the age and maturity of the student and whether the situation in which the consent was given seemed voluntary or coercive.

8. Can educators ask the school-resource officer to search a student's backpack?

Yes, if the educator has reasonable suspicion that the student has committed a crime or violated a school rule (e.g., a teacher smells marijuana or sees a knife in a student's backpack).

Resource Material

Relevant Quotes

The authority possessed by the State to prescribe and enforce standards of conduct in its schools although concededly very broad must be exercised consistently with constitutional safeguards. Among other things, the State is constrained to recognize a student's legitimate entitlement to a public education as a property interest which is protected by the Due Process Clause and which may not be taken away for misconduct without adherence to the minimum procedures required by that clause. . . .

The concern would be mostly academic if the disciplinary process were a totally accurate, unerring process, never mistaken and never unfair. Unfortunately, that is not the case, and no one suggests that it is. . . .

Requiring effective notice and informal hearing permitting the student to give his version of the events will provide a meaningful hedge against erroneous action. At least the disciplinarian will be alerted to the existence of disputes about facts and arguments about cause and effect. He may then determine himself to summon the accuser, permit cross-examination, and allow the student to present his own witnesses. . . . In any event his discretion will be more informed and we think the risk of error substantially reduced. . . .

We have imposed requirements which are, if anything, less than a fair-minded school principal would impose upon himself in order to avoid unfair suspensions.

—Goss v. Lopez (1975)

How should we strike the balance between the schoolchild's legitimate expectations of privacy and the school's equally legitimate need to maintain an environment in which learning can take place? It is evident that the school setting requires some easing of the restrictions to which searches by public authorities are ordinarily subject. The warrant requirement, in particular, is unsuited to the school environment: requiring a teacher to obtain a warrant before searching a child suspected of an infraction of school rules (or of the criminal law) would unduly interfere with the maintenance of the swift and informal disciplinary procedures needed in the schools. . . .

The school setting also requires some modification of the level of suspicion of illicit activity needed to justify a search. Ordinarily, a search . . . must be based on "probable cause" to believe that a violation of the law has occurred . . . [However,] the legality of a search of a student should depend simply on the reasonableness, under all the circumstances, of the search. . . . Under ordinary circumstances, a search of a student by a teacher or other school official will be justified at its inception when there are reasonable grounds for suspecting that the search will turn up evidence that the student has violated either the law or the rules of the school. Such

a search will be permissible in its scope when the measures adopted are rea-
sonably related to the objectives of the search and not excessively intrusive
in light of the age and sex of the student and the nature of the infraction.

—New Jersey v. T.L.O. (1985)

Given the nationwide epidemic of drug use, and the evidence of increased
drug use in Tecumseh schools, it was entirely reasonable for the School
District to enact this particular drug testing policy. . . . The test results
are not turned over to any law enforcement authority. . . . The only con-
sequence of a failed drug test is to limit the student's privilege of partici-
pating in extracurricular activities. . . . Given the minimally intrusive
nature of the sample collection and the limited uses to which the test
results are put, we conclude that the invasion of students' privacy is not
significant. . . .

Within the limits of the Fourth Amendment, local school boards must
assess the desirability of drug testing schoolchildren. In upholding the con-
stitutionality of the policy, we express no opinion as to its wisdom. Rather,
we hold only that Tecumseh's Policy is a reasonable means of furthering
the School District's important interest in preventing and deterring drug
use among schoolchildren.

—Board of Education v. Earls (2002)

The T.L.O. concern to limit a school search to reasonable scope requires the
support of reasonable suspicion of danger . . . before a search can reason-
ably make the quantum leap from outer clothes and backpacks to exposure
of intimate parts. The meaning of such a search, and the degradation its
subject may reasonably feel, place a search that intrusive in a category of
its own.

—Safford Unified School District No. 1 v. Redding (2009)

References

Board of Education v. Earls, 536 U.S. 822 (2002).
Goss v. Lopez, 419 U.S. 565 (1975).
Ingraham v. Wright, 430 U.S. 651 (1977).
Jenkins by Hall v. Talladega City Board of Education, 95 F.3d 1036 11th Cir.
    (1996).
Laney v. Farley, 501 F.3d 577 6th Cir. (2007).
Miranda v. Arizona, 377 U.S. 201 (1966).
New Jersey v. T.L.O., 469 U.S. 325 (1985).
Safford Unified School District No. 1 v. Redding, 129 S.Ct. 2633 (2009).

Additional Resources

Alexander, K., & Alexander, M. D. (2009). *American public school law* (7th ed.). Belmont, CA: Wadsworth. (SEE Chapters 8 and 9)

Fischer, L., Schimmel, D., & Stellman, L. (2010). *Teachers and the law* (8th ed.). Boston: Allyn and Bacon. (SEE Chapter 13)

Russo, C. (2004). *Reutter's the law of public education* (5th ed.). New York: Foundation Press. (SEE Chapter 13)

Thomas, S., Cambron-McCabe, N., & McCarthy, M. (2009). *Public school law: Teachers' and students' rights* (6th ed.). Boston: Allyn and Bacon. (SEE Chapter 7)

Underwood, J., & Webb, L. D. (2006). *School law for teachers.* Upper Saddle River, NJ: Pearson. (SEE Chapter 7)

Student Harassment and Bullying

5

BACKGROUND ON THE ISSUE

Schools have a responsibility to provide a safe educational environment free from peer sexual harassment and bullying. In peer sexual-harassment lawsuits, school boards may be liable for monetary damages if they were deliberately indifferent to peer sexual harassment in the schools. Additionally, many states have passed legislation to prevent bullying in schools. This lesson plan focuses on how school districts can avoid liability in these two areas.

Activator

Motivator

9 min

There are several different clips available on YouTube that discuss harassment and bullying in schools. One very helpful clip can be found at http://www.youtube.com/watch?v=6Wcx2qM5C4g. This YouTube clip is an interview with Diane Sawyer about harassment and bullying in schools. You do not need to play the entire clip. Rather, if you start at minute 1:40 and stop at minute 8:03 within the clip, it would provide a nice introduction to this lesson.

YouTube Screenshot

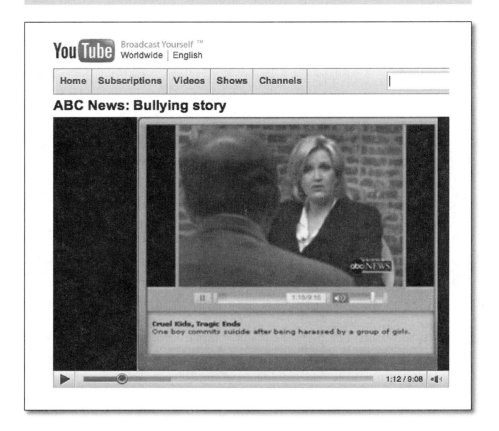

If you are unable to access the clip, please read the following summary:

A popular group of junior high girls began communication via e-mail with a boy with special needs who attended their school. Within these communications, they acted like they had a crush on the boy, when in reality they did not. When the boy finally got up the nerve to ask one of them to the homecoming dance, she responded by saying "No. I would not go to homecoming with you. You are such a retard. My God." Shortly after receiving this message, the boy committed suicide.

Principals will lead a discussion on the Diane Sawyer episode from the YouTube clip. If a YouTube clip is not used, the questions below would still apply to the summary of the clip provided above. Some questions that may guide this discussion include

Could the school district be liable for the cyberbullying in this case?

Could the girls be liable?

Is anyone liable?

Or, is this suicide just the unfortunate result of adolescent cruelty?

Rationale

Objectives

Rationale

3 min

Studies have indicated that as many as 80% of students experience some form of sexual harassment in public schools (American Association of University Women, 2001). Research suggests that such bullying is even more prevalent than peer sexual harassment (Springer, 2008). These statistics are troublesome considering that peer sexual harassment and bullying can have long-term psychological effects on student victims. Indeed, harassment and bullying are serious problems that may impact some students' academic achievement and social well being.

Objectives

Post and/or state the following objectives for the lesson plan:

1. Teachers will be able to apply the legal standard to real-life situations that have occurred in U.S. public schools to determine school-board liability for peer harassment.

2. Teachers will be able to avoid school district liability in peer harassment cases that occur in their classrooms.

3. Teachers will become familiar with trends in antibullying state legislation.

The Law

20 min

To help teachers understand the laws associated with student harassment and bullying, you will have them engage in a think, pair, share activity. To begin, divide all the teachers into two large groups. Assign one group the Davis Case and the other the Indiana legislation. Provide the Davis and Indiana handouts to each group. Next, ask teachers to read their case individually and to *think* about what the case means in regard to the law. Then, ask teachers to *pair* with a member of their group to discuss the implications of what they learned to their practice. Finally, ask teachers to *share* the law and the implications with a member of the other group. The principals can bring the whole group back together to discuss the process.

DAVIS CASE HANDOUT

paper copies

The responsibility of school districts to take action against peer sexual harassment was recognized in the U.S. Supreme Court decision, *Davis v. Monroe County Board of Education* (1999). The Court explained in *Davis* that school officials have clear responsibilities to respond to peer sexual harassment in public schools. When school officials are *deliberately indifferent* to the sexual harassment, school districts can be held financially liable.

Most of the recent peer sexual harassment lawsuits, including the *Davis* decision, have been based on Title IX of the Education Amendments of 1972, which prohibits sex discrimination under any education program or activity receiving federal financial assistance. Title IX has been interpreted broadly to cover peer harassment, and it also includes cases involving teachers harassing students. It is important to note that state laws may also address obligations regarding sex discrimination in schools.

In *Davis* (1999), a fifth-grade female student was allegedly subjected to a prolonged pattern of sexual harassment. According to the complaint, the offending male student attempted to touch the female student's breasts and genital area and made vulgar comments toward her. Additionally, in one incident, the male student placed a doorstop in his pants and acted in a sexually aggressive manner with the female student. The female student and her mother notified a coach, several teachers, and the principal about the various incidents of harassment throughout the school year. School officials, however, failed to effectively respond to these complaints and only threatened possible action. Based on the female student's dropping grades and a suicide note, her mother contended that the continued harassment and the school's failure to respond affected her daughter's education.

In examining this issue, the Supreme Court established a standard of school-district liability for peer sexual harassment under Title IX (1972). In addition to the harassment being based on sex, the following four factors must be present for a school district to be found liable for peer sexual harassment:

1. Appropriate school officials must have *actual knowledge* of the harassment.

2. School officials must have responded with *deliberate indifference* to the harassment (e.g., they did not do anything to stop the harassment or their response was *clearly unreasonable*).

3. The harassment must have been *severe, pervasive, and objectively offensive.*

4. The harassment must have had a *negative impact on a student's education.*

When applying these four factors in the *Davis* (1999) decision, the Court found the school district to be liable for peer sexual harassment. It is important to note that all four factors must be proved for a school district to be held liable. For example, in this case, a mere drop in grades would have been insufficient to prove that the harassment was actionable. However, in conjunction with the other three factors in this case, the grades provided evidence of a connection between the offender's conduct and the denial of educational benefits. The plaintiff's claim also relied on the severity of the harassment and the school's knowledge and deliberate indifference to the harassment. It is also important to note that school officials must have control over the harasser and the environment in order to be liable.

INDIANA ANTIBULLYING HANDOUT

Schools also have the responsibility to provide a safe educational environment free from another form of harassment: bullying. Forty-three states have passed antibullying legislation. Bullying is related to teasing, taunting, hitting, and other threatening behavior that may or may not be sexual in nature. Unlike Title IX (1972)—which is a federal law—bullying is governed by state law. An example of Indiana's antibullying legislation (Indiana Safe Schools Fund, 2009) is provided, in part, below.

Indiana's law defines *bullying* as

overt, repeated acts or gestures, including: (1) verbal or written communications transmitted; (2) physical acts committed; or (3) any other behaviors committed; by a student or group of students against another student with the intent to harass, ridicule, humiliate, intimidate, or harm the other student. (IC 20–33–8–0.2)

(Continued)

(Continued)

Indiana's law was passed as part of the safe school initiative and focuses on prevention. While some state laws emphasize disciplinary action against those who bully in schools (e.g., Georgia and New Jersey), other states stress how schools could improve communication to prevent bullying in schools (e.g., New York).

Interestingly, at least nine states have passed cyberbullying laws aimed at curbing harassment through electronic mediums (e.g., MySpace or Facebook). Bullying legislation was motivated, in part, by school shootings that often involved perpetrators who experienced bullying in school. Teachers often confront legal issues on the topics of peer sexual and nonsexual harassment, including bullying. Thus, an understanding of educators' roles and responsibilities under the law is imperative.

Application

Content to Practice

13 min

The principal will split the teachers into groups of three or four. Each group will read and discuss all four scenarios. In so doing, the teachers should apply the *Davis* (1999) standard to determine whether the school district would be legally liable for harassment based on sex. In Table 5.1, ask the participants to circle all the standards that apply to each case.

Table 5.1   Harassment Scenarios and Davis Standards

paper copies

WWW
HTTP://WWW.CORWIN.COM/TEACHI

Scenario	*Davis* (1999) Standard
1. Jane, a sixth-grade student, was subjected to severe and continuous harassment. The harassment began when she was referred to as the "German gay girl" (*Vance v. Spencer County Public School District*, 2000). The harassment continued when another student asked Jane to describe	1. Appropriate school officials must have *actual knowledge* of the harassment. 2. School officials must have responded with *deliberate indifference* to the harassment (e.g., they did not do anything to stop the harassment, or their response was *clearly unreasonable*).

paper copies

Scenario	*Davis* (1999) Standard
oral sex. Jane was also regularly shoved into walls, and her homework was destroyed on several occasions. During one particular bathroom break from class, several boys called Jane names, such as "whore" and "bitch." While doing so, two of the boys held her hands and the other grabbed her hair and started yanking her shirt off. One of the boys stated that he wanted to have sex with her. School officials responded to several such complaints from Jane and her mother by speaking with the boys, but their response was not effective. Specifically, the boys were only spoken to and not punished. After they were spoken to, Jane contended that the harassment grew worse. When the harassment continued throughout the following school year, Jane and her mother filed a complaint, pursuant to the school-harassment policy. The school claimed that it did not have enough information to investigate. Jane was later diagnosed with depression and withdrew from school. She and her mother then filed a lawsuit against the district. Would the school district be held liable in this situation?	3. The harasser's behavior must have been *severe, pervasive, and objectively offensive.* 4. The harassment must have had a *negative impact on a student's education.*
2. Mary, a high school student, was sexually assaulted by two male students (*Doe v. East Haven Board of Education,* 2006). After Mary told school officials that she had been sexually assaulted, the boys called her a "slut, a liar, a bitch, a whore."	1. Appropriate school officials must have *actual knowledge* of the harassment. 2. School officials must have responded with *deliberate indifference* to the harassment (e.g., they did not

(Continued)

(Continued)

Scenario	Davis (1999) Standard
Mary and her mother made repeated complaints to the superintendent, the principal, and the guidance counselor, which the mother felt were ignored. The school officials argued that they provided the female student with a separate room in the guidance office where she could go if she felt uncomfortable. Would the school district be held liable in this situation?	do anything to stop the harassment, or their response was *clearly unreasonable*). 3. The harasser's behavior must have been *severe, pervasive, and objectively offensive*. 4. The harassment must have had a *negative impact on a student's education*.
3. Tom and Sally were high school juniors and classmates. Tom repeatedly asked Sally for a date, and she repeatedly refused. After the third request, Sally complained to her teacher who told Tom to stop bothering Sally. The following week, Tom asked again and tried to kiss Sally. As a result, her mother complained to the principal and asked him to move Tom to another class. Instead, the principal called Tom to his office, ordered him to stop harassing Sally, and warned Tom of consequences if he did not. The following week, Tom kissed Sally, who became extremely upset. As a result, she was enrolled in a private school and sued the school district for failing to prevent the harassment. Should the school be held liable?	1. Appropriate school officials must have *actual knowledge* of the harassment. 2. School officials must have responded with *deliberate indifference* to the harassment (e.g., they did not do anything to stop the harassment, or their response was *clearly unreasonable*). 3. The harasser's behavior must have been *severe, pervasive, and objectively offensive*. 4. The harassment must have had a *negative impact on a student's education*.
4. Mike, a fifth-grade student, teased a classmate, Mark, about his father being in prison. During recess, Mike would say things like, "Your dad is a child molester," and "You are the son of a criminal." Mark was afraid to walk home from school because	1. Appropriate school officials must have *actual knowledge* of the harassment. 2. School officials must have responded with *deliberate indifference* to the harassment (e.g., they did not do anything to stop the harassment, or their response was *clearly unreasonable*).

Scenario	*Davis* (1999) Standard
Mike and his friends had threatened to jump Mark. Mark has started to pretend he is sick to avoid school. His parents are worried about how withdrawn Mark has become. Does this violate Title IX, or is it most likely to fall under antibullying laws?	3. The harasser's behavior must have been *severe, pervasive, and objectively offensive*. 4. The harassment must have had a *negative impact on a student's education*.

Copyright © 2010 by Corwin. Additional materials and resources related to *Principals Teaching the Law: 10 Legal Lessons Your Teachers Must Know* can be found at http://www.corwin.com/teachinglaw.

Principals should use the outcomes in Table 5.2 for each case to drive the discussion. These key points can also be used as a handout or a presentation slide.

Table 5.2 Davis Scenarios: Moderator Answers

Scenario	Outcome
1	The court held in favor of Jane, finding that the sexual harassment was so severe, pervasive, and objectively offensive that it deprived her of access to the educational opportunities provided by the school and that school officials had actual knowledge of the harassment and were deliberately indifferent to the harassment. Because of the numerous complaints to several different school officials, the actual notice factor was clearly met. A jury awarded the student $220,000 in this case.
2	The court found that school officials had acted unreasonably because it took them five weeks to address the harassment. The court also noted that school officials failed to take actions other than speaking to the harassers. The female student was awarded $35,000 in this case for attorney's fees and costs.
3	This scenario is not based on a real case, but the scenario is a common one. In this situation, it may be difficult to prove peer harassment under Title IX (1972). Applying the *Davis* (1999) decision, school officials knew of the harassment but were not deliberately indifferent. It is important to note that even if school

(Continued)

(Continued)

paper copies

Scenario	Outcome
	officials did not do all that they should have, they still may not be found to be deliberately indifferent if their response was not clearly unreasonable. The third prong of the *Davis* test will be the most difficult to demonstrate. To illustrate, it is not clear whether the harassment in this case was severe, pervasive, or objectively offensive. It is also unclear if the harassment denied Sally her education. Therefore, it does not appear that there has been a violation of Title IX in this scenario. Nevertheless, school officials should still pay attention and respond to such incidents of harassment.
4	Although this would not rise to the level of a Title IX (1972) violation, it may violate a state's antibullying legislation. As noted, bullying legislation varies greatly from state to state.

Assessment

5 min

Delta Cards are a useful assessment activity. *Delta* is Greek for change; here, we are seeking to understand if participants have a new understanding of student harassment and bullying. Ask the teachers to finish the sentence on each card to assess their understanding of the content.

| Figure 5.1 | Harassment and Bullying Assessment Delta Cards |

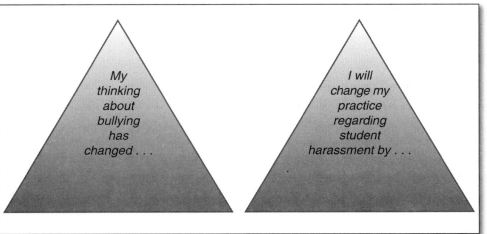

My thinking about bullying has changed . . .

I will change my practice regarding student harassment by . . .

FAQ

10 min

As time permits, you may add some of these additional questions to the follow up discussion.

1. **The *Davis* (1999) case focused on Title IX (1972). Isn't Title IX about gender equity?**

   Yes. Title IX prohibits sex discrimination at educational institutions that receive federal funds. The court has used Title IX in cases involving discrimination based on sex in both student-to-student sexual harassment cases and teacher-to-student sexual harassment cases.

2. **Is same-sex harassment actionable under Title IX (1972)?**

   Yes. The guidance from the Office for Civil Rights states that sexual harassment directed at gay and lesbian students is prohibited under Title IX.

3. How do the courts define *deliberate indifference* and the other factors required to prove liability for peer harassment?

Prior to the *Davis* (1999) decision, it was not clear whether school officials could be liable at all for peer sexual harassment. After the decision, there is much more guidance in this area. Although the *Davis* decision offers some guidance regarding the four factors discussed above, there has been some confusion in interpreting the precise meaning of the factors. For example, which school official needs to have "actual knowledge" of the harassment? Generally, any school official who has the authority to address the harassment will suffice. Or, what constitutes "deliberate indifference"? Some courts have found school officials to be deliberately indifferent when their response is "clearly unreasonable." What may be considered clearly unreasonable is not always clear, however. Finally, when is a harasser's behavior considered "severe, pervasive, and objectively offensive" enough to require action? When determining the severity, courts generally consider the totality of the circumstances.

4. Does Title IX (1972) apply in lawsuits where a teacher harasses a student?

Yes. In order for a school district to be liable for this type of harassment, the school officials must have known about the harassment and must have been deliberately indifferent in responding to the harassment. Even if the school is not liable, the teacher may be found criminally guilty for student harassment.

5. What is the legal standard when an administrator harasses a teacher?

Title VII of the Civil Rights Act of 1964 is the legal standard used in these types of cases. Title VII requires school officials to address the sexual harassment of employees. The sexual harassment against employees usually falls under quid pro quo harassment or a hostile work environment. *Quid pro quo* refers to giving something in order to receive something. For example, a teacher may be promised to be appointed department head in return for sexual favors. A hostile work environment refers to a severely hostile environment that interferes with a teacher's work performance. For example, when an administrator's sexual remarks are severe enough to negatively impact the working environment, the court would find it a hostile work environment.

6. How can school officials avoid harassment in schools?

School districts should create clear sexual harassment policies that provide specific procedures. In addition to promptly dealing with claims of peer sexual harassment, school districts should implement preventive measures, and school administrators and their staff members should ensure that they know and follow those guidelines. To do so, school districts should clearly define peer sexual harassment in student handbooks and share the information with parents. These policies should be discussed to encourage students to report peer harassment immediately to the appropriate school official who is trained in the complaint procedure and has the authority to take corrective action. In addition to handbooks, school districts should provide inservice sessions for faculty and staff members and hold assemblies for students to review complaint procedures. Within the training sessions, it is also important for faculty and students to learn what sexual harassment is, what its effects are, and how to effectively respond to the harassment. Finally, lessons on sexual harassment could be incorporated into the curriculum. It is important not to overreact and to be conscious of the rights of the accused.

7. How many states have passed antibullying legislation?

As of 2010, 43 states have passed antibullying legislation. This number is likely to increase, as other states are considering similar legislation.

8. Which states have passed antibullying legislation?

Alabama, Alaska, Arkansas, Arizona, California, Colorado, Connecticut, Delaware, Florida, Georgia, Idaho, Illinois, Indiana, Iowa, Kansas, Kentucky, Louisiana, Maine, Maryland, Massachusetts, Minnesota, Mississippi, Nebraska, New Hampshire, New Jersey, New Mexico, Nevada, North Carolina, Ohio, Oklahoma, Oregon, Pennsylvania, Rhode Island, South Carolina, Tennessee, Texas, Utah, Vermont, Virginia, Washington, West Virginia, Wisconsin, and Wyoming.

Supplementary Section

We anticipate that teachers may have several Title IX (1972) related questions (e.g., athletics, single-sex classrooms) that were not covered in this lesson plan. Thus, we have included several examples of other frequently asked questions related to Title IX. Principals should use this supplementary section if time permits.

1. Does Title IX (1972) encourage school districts to cut boys' teams?

No, although some have argued that Title IX requires the elimination of male teams in order to achieve equity in school sports. Instead, facility limitations and budgetary concerns put heavy pressure on educational institutions to cut back their athletic programs, which in some cases results in the loss of male teams in order to move toward gender equity.

2. May girls play on boys' teams or boys play on girls' teams?

Title IX (1972) allows separate teams for girls and boys but does not require it. Separate teams are often created due to differences in physical characteristics and sports preference. Under Title IX, school districts must offer equal athletic opportunities through separate or integrated teams. Although Title IX only allows girls to try out for noncontact boys' teams, states' Equal Rights Amendments usually allow girls to also try out for contact sports when there is no girls' team.

3. What if the boys' baseball team gets new uniforms every year and plays its games on a nice field, but the girls' softball team only gets new uniforms every three years and plays its games on a run-down field?

This situation would arguably be a violation of Title IX (1972). School officials would need to provide for greater gender equity between the two teams.

4. Is instruction segregated by sex permissible?

Yes. The U.S. Department of Education adopted regulations that allow school districts to create single-sex classrooms and schools. In coeducational schools, both sexes must be offered equal educational opportunities, and enrollment in a single-sex class should be completely voluntary. Single-sex schools or courses are permitted, but a substantially equal single-sex or coeducational school for students of the other sex must be available.

5. May school districts require pregnant students to attend another school?

No. The U.S. Department of Education has issued regulations under Title IX (1972) not allowing school districts to discriminate against pregnant students. Requiring pregnant students to attend a separate school would be seen as discriminatory.

6. May gender be considered in hiring teachers?

Sometimes. Some gender-based discrimination is allowed under Title VII. However, there must be a legitimate reason for favoring one gender over another. For example, the school district may hire only a female teacher if the job requires supervising the girls' locker room.

7. Who enforces that school districts comply with Title IX, and how does enforcement work?

To ensure compliance with Title IX, three methods of initiating enforcement exist: (1) complaints, (2) compliance reviews, and (3) lawsuits. Under the first method, a person may file a complaint with the Office for Civil Rights (OCR) alleging gender discrimination in violation of Title IX. The OCR then undertakes an investigation of the school. If the school is in violation and no settlement can be reached, the OCR audits the offending school's sports program and orders it to make any changes necessary to comply with Title IX.

The second enforcement mechanism, compliance review, permits the Department of Education to perform periodic investigations of randomly selected public schools to verify compliance with Title IX. Although no complaint needs to be filed for the OCR to perform a compliance review, compliance reviews can occur after a complaint is filed.

A final alternative enforcing Title IX compliance is to file a lawsuit against the offending school. Although lawsuits are costly and time-consuming, sometimes they are the most efficient way of bringing a school into compliance with Title IX for two main reasons. First, even after a complaint is filed, OCR is not required to implement a full investigation. In contrast, the filing of a lawsuit inevitably will result in an investigation by one or both of the parties. Second, the party who files a complaint with the OCR cannot receive monetary damages even if OCR determines that the school violated Title IX. Conversely, the plaintiff in a lawsuit can obtain monetary damages. Schools are more likely to comply with Title IX if noncompliance is punished with monetary damages. Damages vary widely based on the judge or juries assessment of the seriousness of the injury.

Resource Material

Relevant Quotes

Far from childish pranks, sexual harassment in the school setting consists of serious misconduct that can have a devastating effect on students at the receiving end.

—Verna L. Williams (represented the petitioner
in *Davis v. Monroe County Board of Education*, 1999)

Where the misconduct occurs during school hours and on school grounds, the misconduct is taking place "under" an "operation" of the federal education funding recipient. In these circumstances, the recipient retains substantial control over the context in which the harassment occurs. More importantly, however, in this setting the board of education exercises significant control over the harasser. The nature of the state's power over public schoolchildren is custodial and tutelary, permitting a degree of supervision and control that could not be exercised over free adults . . .

Whether gender-oriented conduct rises to the level of actionable "harassment" depends on a constellation of surrounding circumstances, expectations, and relationships, including, but not limited to, the ages of the harasser and the victim and the number of individuals involved. Courts, moreover, must bear in mind that schools are unlike the adult workplace and that children may regularly interact in a manner that would be unacceptable among adults . . .

"Damages are not available for simple acts of teasing and name-calling among schoolchildren" but rather for behavior "so severe, pervasive and objectively offensive that it denies its victims the equal access to education."

—Davis v. Monroe (1999)

While Justice Kennedy may have characterized this case as teaching "little Johnny a perverse lesson in Federalism," Justice O. Connor rejoined by saying that it "assures that little Mary may attend class."

—*New York Times* (Greenhouse, 1999)

Supplies and Materials

In order to show the YouTube clip, the instructor will need access to the Internet during the lesson, or the You Tube clip can be converted to a number of formats that work offline. One such conversion service can be found at www.zamzar.com. The clip can be converted to many formats. Most computers use MOV or MP4 files. If you use an MP3 format, only an audio file will be converted.

References

American Association of University Women. (2001). *Hostile hallways: Bullying, teasing & sexual harassment in schools.* Washington DC: Author.

Davis v. Monroe County Board of Education, 526 U.S. 629 (1999).

Doe v. East Haven Board of Education, 430 F.Supp.2d 54 (2006).

Greenhouse, L. (1999, May 25). The supreme court: The overview; sex harassment in class is ruled schools' liability. *New York Times.* Retrieved February 24, 2010, from http://www.nytimes.com/1999/05/25/us/supreme-court-overview-sex-harassment-class-ruled-schools-liability.html?pagewanted=1

Indiana Safe Schools Fund, Indiana Code 5-2-10.1-2 (2009).

Springer. (2008). Sexual harassment at school—more harmful than bullying. *ScienceDaily.* Retrieved February 24, 2010, from http://www.sciencedaily.com/releases/2008/04/080423115922.htm

Title IX of the Education Amendments of 1972, 20 U.S.C. sec. 1681 (2006).

Title VII of the Civil Rights Act of 1964, 42 U.S.C. sec. 2000e (2006).

Vance v. Spencer County Public School District, 231 F.3d 253 (2000).

Additional Resources

Alexander, K., & Alexander, M. D. (2009). *American public school law* (7th ed.). Belmont, CA: Wadsworth. (SEE Chapter 9)

Brady, K. P. (2008). Student bullying and harassment in a cyberage: The legal ambiguity of disciplining students for cyberbullying. *International Journal of Educational Reform,* 17(2), 92–106.

Brady, K. P. (2008). Sexual harassment. In C. J. Russo (Ed.), *Encyclopedia of education law* (pp. 749–754). Thousand Oaks, CA: Sage.

Brady, K. P., & Conn, K. (2006). Bullying without borders: The rise of cyberbullying in America's schools, *School Business Affairs,* 72(9), 8–10.

Brady, K. P. (2004). Local school officials' legal duty to protect against gay student harassment: The impact of Nabozny and Flores. *West's Education Law Reporter,* 87(1), 383–387.

Conn, K., & Brady, K. P. (2008). MySpace and its relatives: The cyberbullying dilemma. *West's Education Law Reporter,* 226(1), 1–7.

Eckes, S. (2006). Peer sexual harassment and public schools. *Principal Leadership,* *6*(5), 58–63.

Fischer, L., Schimmel, D., & Stellman, L. (2010). *Teachers and the law* (8th ed.). Boston: Allyn and Bacon. (SEE Chapter 16)

Russo, C. (2004). *Reutter's the law of public education* (5th ed.). New York: Foundation Press. (SEE Chapter 13)

Thomas, S., Cambron-McCabe, N., & McCarthy, M. (2009). *Public school law: Teachers' and students' rights* (6th ed.). Boston: Allyn and Bacon. (SEE Chapter 5)

Teacher Freedom of Expression   **6**

BACKGROUND ON THE ISSUE

Although the U.S. Supreme Court has stated that neither students nor teachers shed their constitutional rights to freedom of expression at the schoolhouse door, school officials may discipline teachers for their expression under certain circumstances. The topic of teacher expression is important because teachers may not be aware that courts permit school districts to place limits on their speech—both in and out of school. For example, if a science teacher voices concern about the misuse of the school district's athletic funds, the teacher's speech would most likely be protected, as the teacher would be speaking as a citizen about a matter of public concern. However, when speaking about a private grievance, a teacher's expression will not be protected under the First Amendment. Also, this teacher's speech would not have been protected if she were found to be speaking pursuant to her official job duties.

Activator

Motivator

5 min

The principal will distribute Table 6.1 to five groups of teachers, who will discuss the scenarios. Teachers will return to these scenarios after they have read more about the status of the law in this area.

Table 6.1 Teacher Freedom of Expression Scenarios

paper copies

WWW
HTTP://WWW.CORWIN.COM/TEACHIN

1. A math teacher wrote a letter to a local newspaper criticizing the school board's elimination of girls' softball. As a result of this criticism, the teacher was disciplined. *Did school officials violate this teacher's First Amendment rights?*

2. A special education teacher claimed that school officials retaliated against her after she voiced concerns about the district not complying with special-education law. *Did school officials violate this teacher's First Amendment rights?*

3. Coworkers had advised a nontenured teacher to keep a journal to document his coteacher's tardiness and other unprofessional conduct that occurred in the classroom. The teacher alleged that after he refused to disclose to the principal the names of the coworkers who suggested that he keep a journal, his contract was not renewed. The teacher alleged that his First Amendment rights had been violated. *Were they?*

4. A nontenured teacher's contract was not renewed because she told her social studies class that she does not support the war in Iraq. The teacher claimed that her First Amendment rights were violated. *Does the teacher have a First Amendment right to tell her students that she opposes the Iraq War in class?*

5. After a nontenured biology teacher was advised not to discuss abortion, she was not reappointed after engaging the class in a discussion about the abortion of Down syndrome fetuses. *Did the teacher have a First Amendment right to discuss this issue in the classroom?*

Copyright © 2010 by Corwin. Additional materials and resources related to *Principals Teaching the Law: 10 Legal Lessons Your Teachers Must Know* can be found at http://www.corwin.com/teachinglaw.

Alternative

As an alternative motivator, principals might choose to play the following YouTube clip: http://www.youtube.com/watch?v=l7ZHx2CzrR0.

This news clip discusses teachers being disciplined for their controversial speech inside the classroom. The clip is nine minutes long, but principals only need to play the first few minutes. This short clip should be used to spark the teachers' interest about teacher speech. The clip could be followed up with a quick group discussion about the extent of teachers' First Amendment rights in public schools.

Rationale

Objectives

3 min

Rationale

In the year following a 2006 Supreme Court decision (*Garcetti v. Ceballos,* 2006) that found no First Amendment protections for public employees speaking pursuant to their job responsibilities, more than 20 cases addressed whether a teacher was speaking about an issue related to his or her job duties. Courts in the majority of these decisions failed to protect the school employee because the courts found them to be speaking pursuant to an official job duty. Teachers need to understand the limits of the First Amendment in protecting and not protecting their rights to free expression inside and outside of the classroom.

Objectives

Post and/or state the following objectives for the lesson plan:

1. Teachers will be able to identify when their expression may be protected or limited under the First Amendment.

2. The teachers will be able to apply the First Amendment analysis to real-life scenarios involving teacher speech both inside and outside the classroom.

3. Teachers will gain new knowledge of likely consequences associated with unprotected speech.

The Law

10 min

Teacher freedom of expression is a tricky topic. To develop content knowledge, we advise that the principal ask the teachers to read the following information prior to the professional development session. Unlike other lessons in this book, more time will be allocated to the question-and-answer portion of the lesson. The principal should lead a discussion on what teachers were confused about in the reading, what they now know, and what they want to learn more about.

TEACHER FREEDOM OF EXPRESSION HANDOUT

paper copies

As a result of a U.S. Supreme Court decision (*Garcetti v. Ceballos,* 2006), when teachers speak, *pursuant to official job duties,* their speech will not be protected under the First Amendment—even if they are speaking about a matter of public concern. Thus, a math teacher who complains to an administrator that the district places a disproportionately low number of minority students in gifted math classes might not be protected under the First Amendment (if the teacher is found to be speaking pursuant to his or her job responsibilities). If the teacher is not found to be speaking pursuant to job responsibilities but rather is found to be speaking as a citizen about a *matter of public concern,* the speech may be protected. Specifically, speech that is related to a matter of public concern is protected unless the speech is (1) found to impair teaching effectiveness, (2) interferes with the relationship with superiors or coworkers, or (3) jeopardizes the operation of the school. In applying the *Pickering* (1968) *balancing test,* courts weigh the teacher's rights to freedom of expression against the school district's interest in maintaining an efficient school system. For example, in *Pickering v. Board of Education,* when a teacher wrote a letter to the newspaper criticizing the way school district funds were used, the Court weighed the teacher's rights to free expression against the school district's interest in maintaining an efficient system. In making this determination, the *content of the speaker's statement* should be assessed to determine if the speech impaired one's teaching effectiveness or other *Pickering* factors. The Court did not find that Pickering's letter impaired his teaching effectiveness or other factors, such as interfering with his relationship with superiors or coworkers or jeopardizing the operation of the school.

Regarding expression that occurs inside the classroom, courts have generally upheld restrictions on teachers expressing their personal views. In so doing, courts have noted that *teachers are hired to teach the curriculum.* Thus, school boards may prescribe what will be taught and can restrict how it will be taught as long as the specifications are based on legitimate pedagogical reasons. In addition, *school officials may restrict the use of certain teaching methods,* if the teacher is given proper notice. Furthermore, teachers may not use their classrooms to promote their personal agendas. Thus, when dealing with controversial issues in the curriculum, *teachers are expected to present both sides* and to encourage students to make up their own minds. Teachers have more freedom of expression outside of the classroom, but under certain circumstances, this speech may also be curtailed. For example, if a teacher voices her support for the use of medical marijuana outside of the classroom, this teacher's speech could not be curtailed unless there was evidence that the speech impaired her teaching effectiveness, interfered with relationships to superiors or coworkers, or jeopardized the management of the school. Again, the content of the statements should be assessed in this situation. Although highly unlikely, it is possible in weighing these different interests that school officials might be able to curtail her speech if there was strong evidence that her speech jeopardized the management of the school.

It should also be noted that whether speaking inside or outside the classroom, nontenured teachers have fewer protections than tenured teachers. Specifically, tenured teachers are entitled to due-process rights, making dismissal based on First Amendment concerns more difficult. Indeed, teachers should be knowledgeable about the legal parameters regarding speech both inside and outside the classroom and about the different consequences for tenured teachers compared to nontenured teachers.

Alternative

Specific terms can be extracted from the reading, and the Frayer Diagrams used in Chapter 4 can be implemented.

Application

Content to Practice

15 min

Ask the groups of teachers to revisit the real-world scenarios from the Activator/Motivator. Provide each group with the court-ruling card in Table 6.2 that corresponds with the scenario they previously discussed. Give each group a few minutes to clarify their initial assumptions. Next, ask a representative from each group to read their scenario and the court ruling.

Table 6.2	Freedom of Expression Court-Ruling Cards

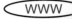

Scenario	Court Ruling
1	The Court found that the teacher was speaking as a citizen. The Court also held that he was speaking about a matter of public concern and that his speech did not interfere with school operations. Thus, the teacher's speech was protected under the First Amendment (see *Pickering v. Board of Education*, 1968).
2	The court found that the special education teacher was speaking pursuant to her official job duties and that her speech was not protected under the First Amendment (see *Houlihan v. Sussex Technical School District*, 2006). The court did find, however, that Section 504 of the Rehabilitation Act, which prohibits retaliation, might protect the teacher in this instance. Thus, even though a teacher may not have a First Amendment right to voice concerns, the teacher may be able to rely on other antiretaliation laws. Some of these antiretaliation laws are addressed later in this lesson plan.
3	The court did not find that the teacher's journal was written pursuant to his official job duties because he was not employed by the district to document the conduct of teachers in the school. The court also found that the teacher's information in the journal was related to a matter of public concern and is protected. Thus, the teacher's speech was protected under the First Amendment (see *Wilcoxon v. Red Clay Consolidated School District*, 2006).
4	The court decided that the teacher was hired to teach the curriculum and that she had no First Amendment rights to voice her personal opinions about the war in class (see *Mayer v. Monroe County Community School Corporation*, 2007). Of significance was that the teacher was told by school officials that she could teach arguments about Iraq from all perspectives, as long as "she kept her opinions to herself."
5	The court found that the teacher's speech could be regulated if the reason for regulation was related to a legitimate pedagogical concern. The court noted that this teacher had been provided with notice of what conduct was prohibited in the classroom (see *Ward v. Hickey*, 1993).

Assessment

7 min

Hand out or present the following scenario and feedback sheet about a foreign-language program. Ask teachers to think about whether the teacher's First Amendment rights were violated. After reading the scenario, ask them to answer the set of questions provided.

TEACHER FREE-SPEECH HANDOUT

A high school French teacher who was the chair of the foreign language department for her district wrote a letter to the editor of a local newspaper criticizing the district for cutting the elementary school foreign language programs. In her letter, she noted that if the district had not been so irresponsible in the management of its athletic funds, it would have been able to keep the elementary school foreign language program in place. After the letter was published, the principal of the high school assigned a new chair to the foreign language department and removed the French teacher from the school policy–council committee. The teacher alleged that the principal violated her rights to free expression under the First Amendment when he retaliated against her for writing the newspaper article. Did the principal violate the teacher's First Amendment rights?

Table 6.3 Free-Speech Assessment

Question	Notes
1. Does this teacher have a valid First Amendment claim?	

(Continued)

(Continued)

Question	Notes
2. Was this teacher speaking pursuant to her official job duties? If not, was the teacher speaking about a matter of public concern or about a private grievance?	
3. What if the teacher in this scenario had been a math teacher complaining about cuts to the elementary foreign language program?	

The principal can lead a short discussion to ascertain the learning of the content. In so doing, the principal will stress that the French teacher's First Amendment rights were most likely not violated in the above scenario. Because it was a French teacher who complained about the cuts to the elementary foreign language program, she would most likely be perceived to speaking pursuant to her official job duties (instead of as a citizen). Therefore, the principal's decision to remove the French teacher from the department chair position and from the policy council would likely be upheld in court even though her comments were arguably related to a matter of public concern. Had the teacher in the scenario taught math, courts would most likely not find the teacher to be speaking pursuant to his or her official job duties. Thus, a math teacher's comments would most likely be considered a matter of public concern and would be protected (unless the speech was found to impair teaching effectiveness, interfere with relationships with superiors, or jeopardize the management of the school).

FAQ

10 min

As time permits, you may add some of these additional questions to the follow up discussion.

1. **When are teachers' statements considered private grievances?**

   When teachers speak on matters of personal interest instead of a matter of public concern, their speech will not be considered protected. For example, one court found that it was a private grievance when a teacher complained about her overcrowded classrooms because she failed to link her argument to matters of public safety (*Cliff v. Board of School Commissioners of the City of Indianapolis*, 1994).

2. **When are teachers' statements considered matters of public concern?**

   Speech will be considered a matter of public concern when it relates to political, social, or other community concerns.

3. **Do teachers have a First Amendment right to post material in their classrooms that expresses their personal viewpoints on controversial matters?**

   Generally no. The courts have upheld the censorship of such materials because teachers are hired to speak for the school district, through the teaching of the district-approved curriculum, not to use their position as teachers to promote their personal views.

4. Is it easier to dismiss a nontenured teacher for his or her classroom expression?

Yes. In most states, nontenured teachers are not entitled to due-process procedures unless they are dismissed during the calendar year. In most states, school officials may choose to not renew a nontenured teacher's contract without offering a reason. On the other hand, tenured teachers are entitled to due-process rights, which could make dismissal much more difficult. It is important to note, however, that when school officials choose not to renew a nontenured teacher's contract, even though they often do not need to give a reason for the nonrenewal, school officials may not retaliate for a nontenured teacher's exercise of constitutionally protected speech.

5. Can school districts offer additional protections to teachers to allow for greater freedom of expression in schools?

Yes. School officials could craft districtwide policies that offer greater freedom of expression in schools. Also, some collective bargaining agreements may address this topic.

6. Are there any state or federal laws that teachers could rely on for protections in these types of cases?

Probably. Most states have adopted whistle-blower laws to protect public employees from retaliation when voicing concerns about illegal activity in the workplace. There are federal whistle-blower laws too. However, both state and federal whistle-blower laws are not as comprehensive as the First Amendment had been before the 2006 U.S. Supreme Court *Garcetti v. Ceballos* (2006) decision. For example, Indiana's whistle-blower law (See McCarthy & Eckes, 2008) states that "a public employer may not terminate an employee for reporting in writing a violation of law or misuse of public resources." However, these laws vary by state. In Wisconsin, for example, an employee

> may not be retaliated against for disclosing information regarding a violation of any state or federal law, rule or regulation, mismanagement or abuse of authority in state or local government, substantial waste of public funds or a danger to public health or safety. An employee may disclose information to any other person. However, before disclosing information to anyone other than an attorney, collective bargaining representative

or legislature, the employee must do one of the following: disclose the information in writing to the employee's supervisor, or disclose the information in writing to an appropriate governmental unit designated by the Equal Rights Division. (Wisconsin Statute, 230.80-85, 2008)

Regarding federal law, Congress has passed federal laws protecting whistleblowers, but these laws would not apply to state employees (See McCarthy & Eckes, 2008). There are, however, other federal protections for claims of retaliation within certain contexts. To illustrate, under Title IX school officials may not retaliate against teachers for complaints related to sex discrimination. Under the Americans with Disabilities Act and Section 504 of the Rehabilitation Act, school officials may not retaliate against teachers for complaints related to disability.

7. How should teachers deal with the teaching of controversial material?

Similar to the scenario discussed above, teachers should present both sides of the issue without inserting their personal viewpoints.

Related Questions and Answers

1. May a teacher, as a parent, challenge the school district's curriculum?

Yes. A teacher, acting as a citizen, may challenge school policies or curriculum and be protected by the First Amendment. This issue could get complicated, however, if the comment was related to the teacher's specific job duties.

2. If a teacher voices her support for gay marriage on a radio show, may school officials discipline this teacher?

No. This teacher would most likely be considered speaking as a citizen and about a matter of public concern. Thus, her expression would be protected, unless the speech impaired her teaching effectiveness.

3. What have the courts said about parental challenges to the curriculum?

The courts have generally not allowed parental disapproval of instructional materials to dictate what is taught in the classroom. The school board maintains control over curricular material.

Resource Material

Relevant Quotes

Although the First Amendment's protection of government employees extends to private as well as public expression, striking the Pickering balance in each context may involve different considerations. When a teacher speaks publicly, it is generally the content of his statements that must be assessed to determine whether they in any way either impeded the teacher's proper performance of his daily duties in the classroom or . . . interfered with the regular operation of the schools generally.

—Givhan v. W. Line Consolidated School District (1979)

Our holding likewise is supported by the emphasis of our precedents on affording government employers sufficient discretion to manage their operations. Employers have heightened interests in controlling speech made by an employee in his or her professional capacity. Official communications have official consequences, creating a need for substantive consistency and clarity. Supervisors must ensure that their employees' official communications are accurate, demonstrate sound judgment, and promote the employer's mission.

—Garcetti v. Ceballos (2006)

The question of whether an employee speaks pursuant to his official duties is not always easy and Garcetti sets forth no dispositive test. Noting, however, that the test should be "a practical one," the U.S. Supreme Court states that formal job descriptions often bear little resemblance to the duties an employee actually is expected to perform.

—Caruso v. Massapequa Union Free School District (2007)

We specifically warned in our amicus brief in the Garcetti case that its implications were potentially far-reaching. The central flaw in Garcetti is the failure to recognize that often great public interest lies in giving government employees broad latitude to speak in the areas of their expertise. In a sense Garcetti got it backwards.

—Robert M. O'Neil, founder of the Thomas Jefferson Center for the Protection of Free Expression (Hudson, 2007)

Supplies and Materials

In order to show the YouTube clip, the instructor will need access to the Internet during the lesson, or the YouTube clip can be converted to a number of formats that work offline. One such conversion service can be found at www.zamzar.com. The clip can be converted to many formats. Most computers use MOV or MP4 files. If you use an MP3 format, only an audio file will be converted.

References

Americans with Disabilities Act of 1990, 42 U.S.C. sec. 12101 (as amended 2008).

Caruso v. Massapequa Union Free School District, 478 F.Supp.2d 377 (E.D.N.Y. 2007).

Cliff v. Board of School Commissioners of the City of Indianapolis, 42 F.3d 403 (7th Cir. 1994).

Garcetti v. Ceballos, 547 U.S. 410 (2006).

Givhan v. W. Line Consolidated School District, 439 U.S. 410 (1979).

Houlihan v. Sussex Technical School District, 461 F.Supp.2d 252 (2006).

Hudson, D. L., Jr. (2007). *Garcetti's palpable effect on public employee speech.* First Amendment Center. Retrieved February 24, 2010, from http://www.first amendmentcenter.org/analysis.aspx?id=18606

Mayer v. Monroe County Community School Corporation, 474 F.3d 477 (2007).

McCarthy, M., & Eckes, S. (2008). Silence in the hallways: The impact of *Garcetti v. Ceballos* on public school educators. *Boston University Public Interest Law Journal, 17*(2), 209–235.

Pickering v. Board of Education, 391 U.S. 563 (1968).

Section 504 of the Rehabilitation Act of 1973, 29 U.S.C. sec. 794 (2000).

Title IX of the Education Amendments of 1972, 20 U.S.C. sec. 1681 (2006).

Ward v. Hickey, 996 F.2d 448 (1993).

Wilcoxon v. Red Clay Consolidated School District, 437 F.Supp.2d 235 (2006).

Wisconsin Statute, 230.80-85 (2008).

Additional Resources

Alexander, K., & Alexander, M. D. (2009). *American public school law* (7th ed.). Belmont, CA: Wadsworth. (SEE Chapter 15)

Fischer, L., Schimmel, D., & Stellman, L. (2010). *Teachers and the law* (8th ed.). Boston: Allyn and Bacon. (SEE Chapter 10)

Russo, C. (2004). *Reutter's the law of public education* (5th ed.). New York: Foundation Press. (SEE Chapter 12)

Thomas, S., Cambron-McCabe, N., & McCarthy, M. (2009). *Public school law: Teacher' and student' rights* (6th ed.). Boston: Allyn and Bacon. (SEE Chapter 9)

Underwood, J., & Webb, L. D. (2006). *School law for teachers.* Upper Saddle River, NJ: Pearson. (SEE Chapter 3)

Teacher Lifestyle Choices and Out-of-School Conduct

7

BACKGROUND ON THE ISSUE

The history of education in the United States is replete with examples of stringent ordinances and school board regulations mandating a higher standard of conduct for teachers than for other community members. Such regulations were enacted because teachers are considered to hold a special position of trust and responsibility due to their relationship with the community's children. Even teachers' actions away from school are judged as if their conduct would set an example for how students should act. In some cases, teachers have been dismissed from schools because of their lifestyle choices. School boards often cite immoral behavior, unprofessional conduct, or unfitness to teach when teachers are dismissed for their out-of-school conduct. However, many teachers argue that their personal conduct outside of school is their own business. This lesson plan addresses the circumstances in which school boards may dismiss teachers for their out-of-school conduct or lifestyle choices.

Activator

Motivator

There are several different clips available on YouTube that discuss teacher lifestyle choices. One very helpful clip can be found at http://www.youtube.com/watch?v=Tc3rMW_JBQo. If you are unable to access this clip, you can summarize the story.

7 min

Video Summary

In this clip, a biology teacher alleges that she was dismissed because of her part-time job. The teacher worked for a charter-boat company that took tourists out to catch fish. While on the boat, the teacher and the other female employees wore bikinis. School officials decided not to renew her contract, and the teacher claimed that it was because she wore a bikini.

Principals will lead a discussion on the bikini YouTube clip based on the questions below (the questions still apply if teachers only heard the summary and did not watch the clip).

- May school officials dismiss teachers for their lifestyle choices or out-of-school activities?
- Was it appropriate for school officials to not renew this teacher's contract based on her lifestyle choices?
- Are there certain types of lifestyles that school officials should monitor more than others?
- Are teachers role models for students? Do they teach by their behaviors in school and by their public actions outside of school?

Rationale

Objectives

Rationale

School officials and teachers are often unsure about whether it is permissible to dismiss teachers because of their lifestyle choices. This lesson plan will help clarify the law in this area.

3 min

Objectives

Post and/or state the following objectives for the lesson plan:

1. Teachers will be able to apply the legal standard to real-life situations that occur in U.S. public schools in examining discipline based on lifestyle choice.

2. Teachers will be able to identify equal-protection and privacy arguments in lifestyle cases.

3. Teachers will be able to discuss trends in lifestyle cases.

The Law

Give the teachers about seven minutes to read the selection below. Then, use the set of presentation slides (Table 7.1) to lead a discussion.

20 min

TEACHER LIFESTYLE CHOICES

State statutes and/or collective-bargaining agreements identify the reasons why teachers may be dismissed. Although the laws vary by state, state laws often include *immorality, unfitness to teach, and unprofessional conduct,* as well as incompetence and insubordination as reasons for dismissal. A school board must show cause in order to dismiss a teacher who has attained tenure. Specifically, in demonstrating cause, the school board must identify under what category of the state's teacher dismissal law a teacher is being dismissed (e.g., immoral conduct, unprofessional conduct).

Interestingly, there is no national standard about what constitutes immoral or unprofessional conduct. The interpretation of these concepts often varies according to state court rulings and community standards. Behavior that could cause substantial disruption in one community may cause little notice in another. In addition to state-law variations, these concepts also vary over time. As the California Supreme Court observed, "Today's morals may be tomorrow's ancient and absurd customs" (*Morrison v. State Board of Education,* 1969).

When making a decision about the appropriateness of a teacher's lifestyle choice, the courts generally consider *the notoriety of the conduct and the impact the conduct has on the individual's teaching abilities.* Courts usually require evidence of a *nexus* (i.e., direct connection) between the teacher's conduct and impaired teaching effectiveness in order for the teacher's dismissal to be justifiable. For example, school officials might be able to discipline a teacher who is a stripper on the weekends if her stripping job became notorious in the community and had a negative impact on her teaching effectiveness. In dismissing this teacher, the school board would, of course, also need to identify a cause for dismissal (e.g., immorality or unprofessional conduct.)

In the past, school districts tried to discharge teachers because of pregnancy or even divorce. Although a few school districts were successful in these types of cases, courts today do not support such dismissals based on their recognition that decisions pertaining to marriage and parenthood involve constitutionally *protected privacy rights.* Similarly, compelled leaves of absence for pregnant, unmarried employees also have been invalidated as violating constitutional privacy rights. For example, at least one court has held that offering a single teacher parental leave without a guarantee of her position upon return violates the teacher's constitutional and statutory rights (see *Ponton v. Newport News School Board,* 1986). Likewise, a Florida court overturned a school board's termination of a teacher for lacking good moral character based on a personal romantic relationship (see *Sherburne v. School Board,* 1984). In this case, the school district questioned her choice as an unmarried woman to spend the night with an unmarried man.

It is also important to note that many teacher-dismissal cases related to teacher lifestyle choices never enter court. For example, a school district recently dismissed a teacher who had appeared in pornographic movies 10 years before becoming a teacher, and the teacher did not challenge the school board's reasoning that her prior conduct would have a negative impact on her classroom effectiveness.

School boards have an easier time dismissing teachers who have engaged in *criminal conduct* outside of the classroom (e.g., drug violations). In one case, a teacher was dismissed for possessing marijuana and for smoking it in his home. The school board relied on a North Carolina law that permits a tenured teacher to be dismissed for "nonmedical use of a controlled substance." The school board upheld his dismissal even though he was never criminally charged by the police (see *In re Freeman,* 1993). In another case, a teacher who brought a loaded shotgun and a loaded pistol to a local poolroom was dismissed for immorality (*Barringer v. Caldwell County Board of Education,* 1996). The court affirmed his dismissal because it found the teacher's conduct to be not only immoral but also highly dangerous. The court reasoned that the teacher's out-of-school conduct violated important principles that are required in the teaching profession. Similarly, an outstanding industrial-arts teacher's dismissal was upheld after he was convicted of aggravated assault with a gun (*Skripchuk v. Austin,* 1977). And in Minnesota, a business teacher was dismissed for unprofessional conduct after being convicted for theft from a company he ran with two other teachers (*In re Shelton,* 1987).

Most recently, the lifestyles of gay, lesbian, bisexual, and transgender (GLBT) teachers have been under scrutiny in some school districts. In a California case, fellow teachers and administrators subjected an award-winning high school biology teacher to years of harassment and allegedly passed her over for promotion because of her lifestyle choice. The California Court of Appeals found that a state labor law *protected* the teacher *from harassment and discrimination based on her sexual orientation* (see *Murray v. Oceanside Unified School District*, 2000).

Similarly, a federal court in Utah held that the removal of a teacher as the girls' volleyball coach was not justified by the community's negative reaction to her homosexuality (see *Weaver v. Nebo School District*, 1998). The court noted that the community's negative response to her homosexuality was not a job-related basis for her removal. Also, an Ohio federal court awarded a teacher reinstatement, back pay, and damages when it found that his contract was not renewed because of his sexual orientation and not because of his teaching deficiencies, as the school board asserted (see *Glover v. Williamsburg Local School District*, 1998).

When school officials try to demonstrate a nexus between the teacher's sexual orientation and its impact on teaching in these cases, they will most likely be unsuccessful because of privacy issues and equal-protection arguments. Specifically, discrimination against GLBT teachers has been challenged using the *Fourteenth Amendment's Equal Protection Clause* (U.S. Constitutional Amendment XIV, 1868). and some state statutes that grant specific protections to GLBT public employees. Under basic equal-protection analysis, if a school district treats a gay teacher differently from a nongay teacher, it needs to demonstrate at least a rational reason for the different treatment.

In addition to the Equal Protection Clause, the Fourteenth Amendment's Due Process Clause (U.S. Constitutional Amendment XIV, 1868) may arguably provide protection for GLBT teachers. The Fourteenth Amendment requires that "no person be deprived of life, liberty or property without due process of law" (U.S. Constitutional Amendment XIV, 1868). As a result, certain types of governmental limits on individual conduct have been held to unreasonably interfere with important individual rights. This interference has amounted to an unreasonable denial of "liberty." Accordingly, there are certain *protected zones of privacy* (e.g., interracial marriage) where the government should not interfere. Also, approximately 19 states have passed laws protecting GLBT teachers from harassment in schools.

| **Table 7.1** | Teacher Lifestyle Presentation Slides |

Reasons for Dismissal

- Immorality
- Unfitness to teach
- Unprofessional conduct
- Incompetence
- Insubordination

A school board must show cause in order to dismiss a teacher who has attained tenure. To show cause means that school officials demonstrate a legitimate reason to dismiss a teacher. The legitimate reason will fall under one of the categories in the causes/reasons for dismissal list, which is established by the state.

When Employment Decisions Are Based on a Teacher's Lifestyle Choice, the Courts Generally Consider

- The notoriety of the conduct
- The impact the conduct has on the individual's teaching abilities

Courts usually require a nexus between the teacher's conduct and impaired teaching effectiveness in order for the teacher's dismissal to be justifiable.

Protection for the Teacher

The Fourteenth Amendment may provide protection for teachers under:

- The Equal Protection Clause (provides for the equal protection of laws)
- The Due Process Clause (requires that "no person be deprived of life, liberty or property without due process of law")

Application

Content to Practice

15 min

The principal will split the teachers into groups of three or four. Each group will be given 2 of the 4 scenarios in Table 7.2 (the outcomes are to be folded over so the teachers do not see them; they are a resource for the principal during the assessment portion). Within the discussion, the teachers should consider whether it would be permissible to discipline the teacher based on his or her lifestyle choices or out-of-school conduct. Also, teachers should consider whether there has been an equal-protection or privacy violation.

Table 7.2	Teacher Lifestyle Scenarios

paper copies

WWW
HTTP://WWW.CORWIN.COM/TEACHINGLAW

Scenario 1

An elementary school teacher was dismissed for immorality because he had a consensual sexual relationship with a seventeen-year-old high school student. He taught this student when she was at the elementary school. The teacher argued that the student no longer attended the elementary school, that his conduct was not criminal, and that the relationship had not affected his professional duties. *Was the school board's action permissible?*

Outcome

The State Supreme Court in Delaware ruled that the teacher was unfit to teach. The court found that the evidence demonstrated a "sufficient nexus between the undisputed sexual relationship and his fitness to teach." The court found that the public disclosure of the relationship had a detrimental impact on the school.

paper copies

Scenario 2

An art teacher painted different pictures using his buttocks. He posted a video of himself painting this way on YouTube. Although the teacher wore a disguise on the video, the school district still learned of this video and attempted to dismiss him. *Could school officials discipline this teacher?*

Outcome

This teacher could be disciplined if his conduct became notorious in the community and if it had a negative impact on his teaching effectiveness.

paper copies

Scenario 3

An eighth-grade teacher from Oklahoma was planning to take his government class on a three-day field trip to Washington, D.C. After a few of the parents learned that the teacher was gay, they demanded that the teacher not be permitted to chaperone the trip and that a straight teacher accompany the students. School officials removed the gay teacher as a chaperone and he sued, claiming a violation of his rights to equal protection under the Fourteenth Amendment. *Does the teacher have a valid claim?*

Outcome

Yes. School officials could be found to have violated the teacher's equal-protection rights under the Fourteenth Amendment by treating him differently than other similarly situated teachers.

Scenario 4

A high school math teacher who also teaches the school district's driver's education course during the summer was arrested for a DUI. The math teacher was driving home from a school district holiday party. The school board would like to dismiss this teacher for unprofessional conduct. *May the school board do so?*

Outcome

The school board would most likely be able to dismiss this teacher because his out-of-school conduct is related to criminal activity and because he is the driver's education instructor. If he did not teach the driver's education course, it would probably be more difficult for school officials to dismiss him for his out-of-school conduct (even though it was criminal behavior) unless it was a felony. Teachers who are convicted of a felony may be fired without evidence that the serious crime impacts on their classroom effectiveness.

Assessment

5 min

Ask the groups of teachers to partner with another group that had a different set of scenario cards. Have the teachers trade the cards—keeping the outcome section folded over and out of sight. Ask individual teachers to pair up, and have them report to one another what they think the outcome of the scenario is. Feedback about each scenario is provided by the outcome side of the card as well as the teacher partner who had previously discussed the scenario.

FAQ

10 min

As time permits, you may add some of these additional questions to the follow up discussion.

1. **Can teachers be dismissed because of rumors of immoral conduct?**

   No. Teachers can only be dismissed based on factual evidence. At least one court has noted that to discipline a teacher based merely on allegations would create a dangerous precedent (*Fisher v. Snyder*, 1973).

2. **Could a teacher be disciplined for encouraging a student to lie?**

Yes. One court upheld the school's decision to discipline a teacher when he had a student lie about his weight at a wrestling tournament. Such conduct would probably be considered immoral.

3. **How do courts define immoral conduct?**

Immorality or *immoral conduct* has been defined in several different ways. One court noted that "immorality is an imprecise word which means different things to different people. In essence, it connotes conduct not in conformity with accepted principles of right and wrong behavior. It is contrary to the moral code of the community; wicked; especially, not in conformity with the acceptable standards of proper sexual behavior" (*Harry v. Marion City Board of Education*, 1998).

4. **Could a teacher be dismissed for having a sexual relationship with a former student who has recently graduated?**

Most likely. Some courts have permitted the dismissal of a teacher for such relationships. For example, in one case, a high school teacher alleged that school officials violated her rights to privacy and intimate association when they denied her tenure after she engaged in an intimate relationship with a former female student. Affirming the federal district court opinion, the Sixth Circuit held that the school board acted reasonably (see *Flaskamp v. Dearborn Public Schools*, 2004). It would seem that the closer to graduation the relationship began, the more problems a teacher would have defending the relationship.

5. Could a teacher be dismissed for having a nonsexual relationship with a student?

Possibly. Recently in Indiana, a teacher lost her job because she forged too close a friendship with a middle school student. The student's mother complained that they commonly gossiped on the phone for hours about students' sexual lives and other inappropriate topics. This teacher had been warned by school officials about previous close relationships with students and ignored the warnings.

6. May school officials punish a teacher for a posting a picture of herself smoking and drinking a beer on Facebook?

Maybe. Although the teacher may argue that what she does in her private life may not be regulated by school officials, the school officials might still be able to demonstrate that the picture has impaired her teaching effectiveness in the classroom.

7. May school officials discipline a teacher for attending a rally to legalize marijuana?

Most likely not. Although teachers have the right to engage in political activities, school officials have some authority to place restrictions on teachers' political activities that occur inside the school. Activities that occur outside the school, such as the example mentioned above, would be much more difficult to control. Courts have found that teachers have the right of free association and cannot be disciplined for nondisruptive political activities.

> ### Resource Material

Relevant Quotes

A rational nexus exists between a teacher's off-duty conduct and his duties as a teacher in at least two circumstances: (1) if the conduct directly affects the performance of the occupational responsibilities of the teacher; or (2) if, without contribution on the part of the school officials, the conduct has become the subject of such notoriety as to significantly and reasonably impair the capability of the particular teacher to discharge the responsibilities of the teaching position.

—Powell v. Paine (2007)

Immorality as a ground for dismissal must "negatively affect the ability of the teacher to carry out his or her required responsibilities" and that the teacher must have "actual or constructive notice of the moral standard in question," which is satisfied if the teacher should know that the conduct is "universally condemned" or "would cause a strong negative reaction against him in the community."

—Ross v. Springfield School District No. 19 (1986)

In order to dismiss a school board employee for acts performed at a time and place separate from employment, the Board must demonstrate a "rational nexus" between the conduct performed outside of the job and the duties the employee is to perform.

—Rogliano v. Fayette County Board of Education (1986)

If the state may require parents to relinquish their children to the influence of public school teachers on a daily basis, then surely it is reasonable for parents to demand that public school teachers adhere to standards of conduct consonant with the moral standards of the community, especially when such conduct is required by law.

—Rogliano v. Fayette County Board of Education
[Dissenting Opinion] (1986)

While the school board may legitimately inquire into the character and integrity of its teachers, in reviewing the character of a teacher, a nexus between the teacher's conduct and the workings of the educational system must be demonstrated.

—Thompson v. Southwest School District (1980)

Supplies and Materials

In order to show the YouTube clip, the instructor will need access to the Internet during the lesson, or the YouTube clip can be converted to a number of formats that work offline. One such conversion service can be found at www.zamzar.com. The clip can be converted to many formats. Most computers use MOV or MP4 files. If you use an MP3 format, only an audio file will be converted.

References

Barringer v. Caldwell County Board of Education, 473 S.E.2d 435 (1996).
Fisher v. Snyder, 476 F.2d 375, 377 (1973).
Flaskamp v. Dearborn Public Schools, 385 F.3d 935 (2004).
Glover v. Williamsburg Local School District, 20 F.Supp.2d 1160 (1998).

Harry v. Marion City Board of Education, 506 S.E.2d 319, 320 (1998).

In re Freeman, 426 S.E.2d 100 (1993).

In re Shelton, 408 N.W.2d 594 (Minn. Ct. App. 1987).

Morrison v. State Board of Education, 461 P.2d 375 (Cal. 1969).

Murray v. Oceanside Unified School District, 95 Cal. Rptr. 2d 28 (2000).

Ponton v. Newport News School Board, 632 F.Supp. 1056 (1986).

Powell v. Paine, 655 S.E.2d 204, 209 (W. Va. 2007).

Rogliano v. Fayette County Board of Education, 347 S.E.2d 220 (1986).

Ross v. Springfield School District No. 19, 716 P.2d 724 (1986).

Sherburne v. School Board, 455 S0.2d 1057 (Fla. Dist. Ct. App. 1984).

Skripchuk v. Austin, 379 A.2d 1142 (Del. 1977).

Thompson v. Southwest School District, 483 F.Supp. 1170, 1184 (1980).

U.S. Constitutional Amendment XIV (1868).

Weaver v. Nebo School District, 29 F.Supp.2d 1279 (1998).

Additional Resources

Alexander, K., & Alexander, M. D. (2009). *American public school law* (7th ed.). Belmont, CA: Wadsworth. (SEE Chapter 15)

Eckes, S., & McCarthy, M. (2006). Teachers' privacy rights. *National Association of Secondary School Principals, 6*(3), 1–6.

Fischer, L., Schimmel, D., & Stellman, L. (2010). *Teachers and the law* (8th ed.). Boston: Allyn and Bacon. (SEE Chapter 14)

Russo, C. (2004). *Reutter's the law of public education* (5th ed.). New York: Foundation Press. (SEE Chapter 10)

Sugarman, S. (2003). "Lifestyle" discrimination in employment. *Berkeley Journal of Employment and Labor Law, 24*(2), 377–438.

Thomas, S., Cambron-McCabe, N., & McCarthy, M. (2009). *Public school law: Teacher' and student' rights* (6th ed.). Boston: Allyn and Bacon. (SEE Chapter 9)

Underwood, J., & Webb, L. D. (2006). *School law for teachers.* Upper Saddle River, NJ: Pearson. (SEE Chapter 3)

Religion   **8**

BACKGROUND ON THE ISSUE

There may be no constitutional issue in American life more controversial and divisive than the inclusion or prohibition of religion in the public schools. For decades, the controversy has divided parents, teachers, school boards, and the justices of the U.S. Supreme Court. Should public schools begin their day with the recitation of a prayer for all students or for those who want to pray? Can school districts require a moment of silence for prayer or meditation? Can principals invite clergy or students to give invocations at graduation ceremonies? Can students or teachers organize prayer or Bible-study clubs? Can public schools celebrate Christmas? Can students distribute religious pamphlets? Can school districts teach and even require courses about religion? And, can school districts teach scientific creationism or intelligent design in science courses? These are some of the issues that are being debated today and are likely to continue to be debated in the years to come.

What does the Constitution say about these questions? When most citizens think about religion and the Bill of Rights, two phrases come to mind: "Freedom of religion" and "separation of church and state." Although neither of these phrases is in the Constitution, they are a popular way of capturing two phrases that *are* in the First Amendment. The Establishment Clause ("Congress shall make no law respecting an establishment of religion") has been interpreted by Thomas Jefferson to require "a wall of separation between church and state" (*Everson v. Board of Education of the Township of Ewing,* 1947). The clause concerning "the free exercise" of religion has been interpreted to guarantee freedom of religion for all citizens. But, as no provision of the Bill of Rights is absolute, the questions to be resolved by the courts are: Should Jefferson's metaphorical wall of separation continue to guide us today? And if so, how high should the wall be in the public schools? Second, how much freedom of religion must be protected, or at least tolerated, in public schools? This lesson will indicate how the courts have ruled on these important questions and outline court opinions that can guide educators in responding to these sensitive issues.

Activator

Motivator

Ask teachers individually to indicate their opinion about the following proposals or activities in Yourtown: Are they Constitutional? Unconstitutional? Or, you don't know. You may choose to formally or informally tally the participants' responses.

6 min

Table 8.1 Religion Hypothetical Cases

Hypothetical Cases	Constitutional?		
Case 1. The principal of the middle school invites student volunteers to lead the following nondenominational prayer at lunch time over the cafeteria PA system for students who wish to participate: "God is great, God is good, and we thank him for our food."	Yes	No	Don't Know
Case 2. The school board proposes that every school in the district begin the school day with "one minute of silence for prayer or meditation."	Yes	No	Don't Know
Case 3. The high school principal proposes that each year different community clergy give nondenominational invocations at the high school graduation. He adds that no student will be required to participate.	Yes	No	Don't Know
Case 4. A group of students petition the administration to recognize their prayer and Bible-study organization as an official club that will be eligible to publicize their meetings on school bulletin boards and daily announcements and to use school facilities for their activities.	Yes	No	Don't Know

paper copies

WWW
HTTP://WWW.CORWIN.COM/TEACHIN

paper copies

Hypothetical Cases	Constitutional?		
Case 5. The music teacher proposes a Christmas assembly at which the school choir would sing the traditional hymns of the holiday season.	Yes	No	Don't Know
Case 6. The school board issues a new policy that science teachers who teach about the theory of evolution must also teach students about the theory of creation science or intelligent design so that students can make up their own minds about these competing theories concerning human origins.	Yes	No	Don't Know
Case 7. In order to teach an appreciation of different spiritual perspectives, the school board will require all high school students to complete a course in comparative religion (that will include readings from the Bible and the Koran) in order to graduate.	Yes	No	Don't Know
Case 8. A group of fundamentalist Christian parents object to two required elementary school books: One is a novel that they believe promotes witchcraft; the second is a book that comments approvingly of gay marriage. Because the content of these books are in conflict with their basic religious values and beliefs, the parents make two proposals. A: Both books should be eliminated from the curriculum because they are antireligious and/or promote the religion of secular humanism. B: If the books are not banned, the parents argue that compelling their children to read these books violates their free exercise of religion; therefore, the students have a right to be excused from reading the books and be given alternative assignments.	Yes	No	Don't Know
Case 9. On Valentine's Day, Sue Pious wrote on each Valentine she gave to all her classmates, "Jesus loves you." Her third-grade teacher stopped Sue's distribution because, she said, Sue shouldn't be promoting her religious beliefs in public schools.	Yes	No	Don't Know

Rationale

Objectives

Rationale

7 min

Teachers often wonder whether religion-related activities in class are legally permissible (e.g., singing holiday songs, student prayer). With a better understanding of how the courts have interpreted the Free Exercise Clause and the Establishment Clause, teachers will be better equipped to understand what is permissible under the law.

Objectives

Post and/or state the following objectives for the lesson plan:

1. Teachers will be able to identify how the courts have interpreted the Establishment Clause of the First Amendment in cases dealing with conflicts about religious issues in the public schools.

2. Teachers will be able to identify how courts have interpreted the Free Exercise Clause in school cases.

3. Teachers will be able to examine the constitutional principles that emerge from court decisions concerning religion and education that provide guidelines for educators facing those issues in their schools.

4. Teachers will be able to explain the constitutional principles they support and better understand and respect the views about church–state issues with which they disagree.

The Law

15 min

In this lesson, participants will investigate three elements of the law that directly relate to religion in schools: (1) the Establishment Clause, (2) the Free Exercise Clause, and (3) the Equal Access Act. During this time, each teacher should individually make a KWL chart. (This can also be done on the chalkboard or on butcher paper.) The KWL chart asks participants to ask what they *know*, what they *want* to know, and what was *learned*. To begin, teachers will answer what they currently know and what they want to know (the first two parts of the KWL chart). Next, each teacher should silently read the four-page "Religion and School Law" that is distributed. Finally, ask the teachers to complete the final portion of the chart. An example of the KWL chart is included below.

K	What do you *know*?	In other words, what did you already know about this topic before completing this reading.
W	What do you *want* to know	Before reading the four pages, list what you wanted to know about this topic
L	What did you *learn*	After completing the four-page reading, list what you have learned.

After each teacher finishes the KWL chart, the principal will ask groups of teachers (3 to 6) to discuss the commonalities of their KWL charts. Note: principals should guide teachers to focus their time on K (what they know) and L (what they learned). The principals should then have representatives from each group report out in order to determine the commonalities of the larger group.

RELIGION AND SCHOOL LAW

The *First Amendment* proclaims, "Congress shall make no law respecting an establishment of religion or prohibiting the free exercise thereof" (1791). But, it is not obvious what these historic words mean. The answer can be found in the way the federal courts have interpreted the religion clauses over the years and applied them to disputes in the public schools.

In 1947, the U.S. Supreme Court for the first time determined the meaning of the *Establishment Clause*. In *Everson v. Board of Education of the Township of Ewing* (1947), all the justices agreed with Thomas Jefferson that "the clause against establishment of religion by law was intended to erect a 'wall of separation between church and state.'" Despite this unanimous interpretation, a majority of the Justices did not believe that the wall of separation prohibited a school district from reimbursing parents for bus fare for transporting their children to religious as well as public schools.

Over the years, the unanimous support for a wall of separation among the Justices began to erode. For example, in 1971 the High Court dropped the wall metaphor and established the following three-part *Lemon test* for determining whether a challenged government practice was constitutional: First, the activity must have a *secular purpose*;

second, its *primary effect* must be one that *neither advances nor inhibits religion*; finally, the activity must not foster an *excessive government entanglement* with religion. In the *Lemon* case, the Court held that state salary supplements paid to teachers in religious schools violated the three-part test (*Lemon v. Kurtzman,* 1971).

In *Lynch v. Donnelly* (1984), Justice O'Connor developed the *Endorsement test* that was a "refinement" of the test used in *Lemon.* This approach asked two questions: first, "whether government's purpose is to endorse religion" and, second, whether the policy "actually conveys a message of endorsement." In *Lynch,* Justice O'Connor explained that government endorsement of religion is invalid because it "sends a message to nonadherents that they are outsiders, not full members of the political community, and an accompanying message to adherents that they are insiders, favored members of the political community."

A year later, the Court ruled on an Alabama statute that added the words "voluntary prayer" to a law that required schools to begin each day with a minute of silence. The expressed purpose of the law was "to return voluntary prayer to public schools." Therefore, the Court held that the statute clearly violated the secular purpose part of the *Lemon* test because its goal was "to convey a message of state approval of prayer" (*Wallace v. Jaffree,* 1985).

The following decade, the Court confronted the question of whether invocations and benedictions at public school graduations violated the Establishment Clause. In *Lee v. Weisman* (1992), a divided Court struck down the school-sponsored prayers and wrote, "if citizens are subjected to state-sponsored religious exercises, the State disavows its own duty to guard and respect" the diversity of religious belief. This is especially true in public schools, where prayer exercises "carry a particular risk of indirect coercion." Similarly in 2000, the Supreme Court ruled that it was unconstitutional for schools to authorize students to vote on whether invocations should be delivered before football games. In *Santa Fe Independent School District v. Doe* (2000), the Court explained that the Constitution does not prohibit an individual student from praying before, during, or after school. However, the Establishment Clause *is* violated when a public school sponsors or endorses a religious practice, such as organizing an election to select a student to say a prayer at an athletic event. As the Supreme Court explained in an earlier case, the problem with such an endorsement is that "when the power, prestige, and financial support of government are placed behind a particular religious belief, the indirect coercive pressure upon religious minorities to conform to the prevailing officially approved religion is plain" (*Engel v. Vitale,* 1962).

In addition to prohibiting school-sponsored prayers, the courts also prohibit curricular proposals that promote religion. Thus, the Supreme Court voided a law that required schools that teach evolution to also teach "creation science." The law violated the Establishment Clause because it advances a religious doctrine (based on the first chapter of Genesis) "by requiring either the banishment of the theory of evolution from public school classrooms or the presentation of a religious viewpoint that rejects evolution in its entirety" (*Edwards v. Aguillard,* 1987).

While the Establishment Clause prohibits public schools from encouraging religion, the *Free Exercise Clause* protects students in their religious expression. Thus, individual students may say prayers in school and share their religious views with classmates as long as they do not cause disruption. Furthermore, the Free Exercise Clause and the Equal Access Act (1984) permit groups of students to organize religious groups in school. Congress passed the *Equal Access Act* to allow secondary students to form student-led, noncurricular clubs to meet during noninstructional time. The Act was upheld by the Supreme Court in the case of a Christian club that was denied the right to meet at a public school for Bible study and prayer (*Board of Education of the Westside Community Schools v. Mergens,* 1990). The school argued that recognizing a religious group would violate the Establishment Clause. However, the Supreme Court disagreed and upheld the federal Equal Access Act that prohibited discrimination against voluntary student organizations based on their political or religious views. The Court noted that the proposed meetings were voluntary, student initiated, and not sponsored by parents, the school, or its staff. According to the Court, "If a state refused to let religious groups use facilities open to others, then it would demonstrate not neutrality but hostility toward religion." The Court further explained that

> There is a crucial difference between government speech endorsing religion which the Establishment Clause forbids, and private speech endorsing religion which the Free Speech and Free Exercise Clauses protect. We think that secondary school students are mature enough and are likely to understand that a school does not endorse or support student speech that it merely permits. (*Board of Education of the Westside Community Schools v. Mergens,* 1990)

Therefore, the Court ruled that the religious club should be allowed to meet.

Application

Content to Practice

20 min

In small groups, teachers will return to the nine hypothetical cases that were previously examined. The goal is to apply the principles and precedents of the Supreme Court's decisions to determine whether the activities proposed in the cases are constitutional or not and why. Each group will have one moderator who will be given Table 8.2 to bring clarity to the discussion of each case. The principals should make enough copies of this handout to provide to every teacher at the conclusion of the activity.

Table 8.2

paper copies

Case Number	Constitutional?	Why?
1	No	As the Supreme Court explained, it is unconstitutional for government officials to encourage or endorse a religious practice. Therefore, when a public school principal, who is an agent of the government, invites students to say prayers, she is thereby encouraging religion and violating the Establishment Clause. However, as the Court also explained, students are free to say individual prayers at lunch or any other time before, during, or after school as long as they don't cause disruption.
2	Probably Yes	If the school board required "a minute of quiet for silent prayer," this policy would be unconstitutional because it would only encourage prayer as the Supreme Court explained in *Wallace v. Jaffree* (1985). But, a majority of the Justices have indicated that as long as the board does not state that its purpose is religious, and the only activity that is required is silence (for prayer *or* meditation), then students can use that minute of silence for any purpose they wish— whether religious, nonreligious, or even antireligious. Thus, most moment-of-silence policies would be upheld if they have a secular purpose, such as starting the school day with a time for silent reflection.
3	No	As the Court ruled in *Lee v. Weisman* (1992), school-sponsored invocations or benedictions violate the Establishment Clause. The practice is equally unconstitutional if the principal asks a teacher, student, or parent to say the prayer even if participation is voluntary. What makes this practice unconstitutional is that a public school principal, who is an agent of the government, is promoting a religious practice. Thus, the government should be neutral concerning religion—neither endorsing nor inhibiting religion.
4	Yes	Under the federal Equal Access Act (1984), secondary schools that permit extracurricular clubs can't refuse to provide equal access to a group because of its religious or political speech. This would include the use of bulletin boards and other school facilities like any other extracurricular club. Discrimination against a student religious group would also be a violation of the Free Exercise Clause of the First Amendment.

paper copies

Case Number	Constitutional?	Why?
5	Probably Not	How to handle Christmas in a public school can be a delicate matter. One approach is for schools to have "holiday," rather than Christmas, assemblies. But since Christmas is a national as well as a religious holiday, it is not unconstitutional to have a Christmas assembly where the school chorus sings the nonreligious songs of the season. The constitutional problem arises if the chorus only sings traditional Christmas hymns—which typically include explicit religious affirmations. In that case, there would probably be a violation of the Establishment Clause because such an assembly would appear to be an endorsement of religion. This does not mean that students can never sing or be taught about religious music. For example, such music can be taught objectively as part of a course on the history of Western music. But, most judges probably would conclude that a program of religious hymns at a Christmas assembly just before Christmas would constitute an unconstitutional endorsement of religion. (However, the songs might be OK if they were part of a larger, objective curriculum about comparative religious celebrations.)
6	No	As the Supreme Court ruled in the *Edwards* (1987) case, such a policy would violate the Establishment Clause because it promotes a religious view, as it requires schools either to stop teaching evolution or to present a religious view that rejects evolution. Furthermore, creationism is based on the first book of the Bible and rejects scientific methods. Even though intelligent design is a more sophisticated theory than creationism, the proponents and goals of intelligent design are similar to those of creationism, and it has been rejected by a federal court for the same reasons (see *Kitzmiller v. Dover*, 2005).

(Continued)

Table 8.2 (Continued)

Case Number	Constitutional?	Why?
7	Yes	The courts distinguish between courses and activities that *promote* religion, which is unconstitutional, and courses that teach *about* religion, which is permitted and can be required if it is taught objectively as part of the curriculum. Furthermore, reading and teaching about the Bible could be appropriate not just in a course on comparative religion but also in other courses such as literature, history, or music.
8	A: No B: Probably Not	The parents have no constitutional right to require schools to ban books that are in conflict with their religious beliefs as long as schools have a legitimate educational goal in assigning the books. As one federal court explained, if schools were required to eliminate everything objectionable to every parent's religious views, this would "leave public education in shreds" (see *Grove v. Mead*, 1985). In cases such as this, many schools excuse students from classes such as sex education or reading assignments that are in conflict with their religious beliefs and, where feasible, provide alternative assignments. But, most courts have not found "excusal" to be a parental right under the Free Exercise Clause because merely exposing students to controversial ideas does not interfere with the parents' freedom to educate their children in the religion of their choice.
9	No	Sue has a constitutional right to distribute her valentines with her personal message like any other student. The outcome would be entirely different if Sue's teacher distributed valentines to her pupils with the words "Jesus loves you." This is because the teacher's valentines would constitute a government endorsement of religion that is prohibited by the Establishment Clauses. In contrast, Sue's individual religious views are protected by the Free Exercise and Free Speech Clauses of the First Amendment.

Assessment

5 min

At the conclusion of the lesson, ask teachers to use the hand-out to individually record their responses on the two new cases in Table 8.3. Ask the teachers to indicate which constitutional clause applies and then to discuss their responses with the person sitting next to them.

Table 8.3   Religion Assessment

paper copies

HTTP://WWW.CORWIN.COM/TEACHINGLAW

Case	Circle One		Decision and Reasoning
While Gail Good is saying her rosary prayers after lunch in the school cafeteria, her fifth-grade teacher quietly explains to Gail that she should say her prayers in church or at home but not in a public school.	Free Exercise	Establishment Clause Principles	
Sixth-grade teacher Sam Saint gives his students a flyer that announces a special youth prayer service at a local church. He explains that all students are welcome, but they should get their parents' permission to come to the service.	Free Exercise	Establishment Clause Principles	

Answers for Table 8.1

1. The Free Exercise and Free Speech Clauses apply to Good's case. Based on these First Amendment provisions, Gail has the freedom and the right to say her individual prayers in school as long as she doesn't cause disruption.

2. The Establishment Clause applies to Mr. Saint. As an agent of the government, Saint is prohibited from endorsing or encouraging religious activity in his role as a teacher. As his distribution of the flyers announcing a prayer service is an encouragement of religion, it is a violation of the Establishment Clause—even if the parents give their children permission to attend.

Alternative

Read each case and ask teachers to stand at a designated area of the room based on what they think about each case. For example, ask teachers that believe Gail (in the first case) can pray to stand in the back of the room. Have others stand at the front. Then, ask volunteers to provide their rationale. Finally, use the answers provided to clarify any misconceptions. This can be repeated for the second case if time permits.

FAQ

7 min

As time permits, you may add some of these additional questions to the follow-up discussion.

1. **Must students salute the flag or recite the Pledge of Allegiance?**

   No. When children of Jehovah's Witnesses refused to salute the flag or say the pledge for religious reasons, the Supreme Court ruled in their favor. If a majority of the voters want to require these patriotic exercises in schools, why should a small minority be free to ignore that requirement? In answer, the Court wrote:

The very purpose of a Bill of Rights was to withdraw certain subjects from the vicissitudes of political controversy, to place them beyond the reach of majorities and officials and to establish them as legal principles to be applied by the courts. One's right to life, liberty, and property, to free speech, a free press, freedom of worship and assembly, and other fundamental rights may not be submitted to vote; they depend on the outcome of no elections. (*West Virginia v. Barnette*, 1943)

In subsequent cases, courts have ruled that students can refuse to salute the flag or stand for the Pledge—even if they don't have a religious reason—as long as they are not disruptive.

2. Do the words *under God* in the Pledge violate the Establishment Clause?

The question has not been resolved by the Supreme Court. In a recent case, a federal appeals court ruled that the phrase had a religious purpose and conveyed an "impermissible message of endorsement to some and disapproval to others of their beliefs regarding the existence of a monotheistic God." But the Supreme Court overturned the ruling on procedural grounds. Therefore, the High Court has not decided the substantive question of whether the inclusion of "under God" in the Pledge in public schools violates the Establishment Clause (*Elk Grove Unified School District v. Newdow*, 2004). In a more recent federal appeals court decision, the court ruled that reciting the Pledge in school does not violate the Constitution. Perhaps the U.S. Supreme Court will revisit the issue and finally resolve this matter.

3. Can students receive religious instruction during school hours?

Yes. However, this "release time" instruction used by some communities must take place away from school and must not be taught by school staff nor paid for by the school.

4. Can public school teachers do remedial work in religious schools?

Yes. In *Agostini v. Felton* (1997), the Supreme Court ruled that placing public school teachers in parochial schools to conduct remedial instruction does not necessarily result in "state sponsored indoctrination of religion or constitute a symbolic union between government and religion."

5. Are there religious reasons to support church–state separation?

Yes. Since the plaintiffs in some prominent school-prayer cases were atheists, there is a tendency to assume that those who support church–state separation are atheists, agnostics, or antireligious secular humanists. In fact, however, many religious people are "separationists." Some saw separation as a way to protect the churches against state control and worldly corruption. Today, many believers fear that what government promotes and funds, government may control. As Justice Blackman noted in *Weisman,* "religion flourishes in greater purity, without than with the aid of government" (*Lee v. Weisman,* 1992). Furthermore, religious sociologists have found that Americans are more religious than citizens of European countries, where governments financially support churches and schools. Some conclude that the reason for greater popularity of religion in the United States is that as our churches can't depend on government support, they are more responsive, relevant, and creative than European religious institutions.

6. **Why are prayers permitted at presidential inaugurations but not in public schools?**

   While the Supreme Court sometimes seems inconsistent in its Establishment Clause decisions, the Court has always maintained a higher wall of separation in cases involving the public schools. This is because of the central and delicate role of public schools in American life, because students are compelled to attend and because they are at a formative and impressionable age.

Resource Material

Relevant Quotes

If there is any fixed star in our constitutional constellation, it is that no official, high or petty, can prescribe what shall be orthodox in politics, nationalism, religion, or other matters of opinion or force citizens to confess by word or act their faith therein. If there are any circumstances which permit an exception, they do not now occur to us.

—West Virginia v. Barnette (1943)

The First Amendment has erected a wall between church and state. That wall must be kept high and impregnable. We could not approve the slightest breach.

—Everson v. Board of Education of the Township of Ewing (1947)

The political interest in forestalling intolerance extends beyond intolerance among Christian sects—or even intolerance among religions—to encompass intolerance of the disbeliever and the uncertain.

—Wallace v. Jaffree (1985)

Families entrust public schools with the education of their children, but condition their trust on the understanding that the classroom will not purposely be used to advance religious views that may conflict with the private beliefs of the student and his or her family [because] students in such institutions are impressionable and their attendance is involuntary. . . . Consequently, the Court has been required often to invalidate statutes which advance religion in public elementary and secondary schools.

—Edwards v. Aguillard (1987)

There are heightened concerns with protecting freedom of conscience from subtle coercive pressure in the elementary and secondary public schools. [What] to most believers may seem nothing more than a reasonable request that the nonbeliever respect their religious practices, in a school context may appear to the nonbeliever or dissenter to be an attempt to employ the machinery of the State to enforce a religious orthodoxy.

—Lee v. Weisman (1992)

The overwhelming evidence at trial established that ID (intelligent design) is a religious view, a mere re-labeling of creationism, and not a scientific theory. . . . Encouraging the teaching of evolution as a theory rather than as a fact is one of the latest strategies to dilute evolution instruction employed by anti-evolutionists with religious motivations. . . . ID fails to meet the essential ground rules that limit science to testable, natural explanations.

—Kitzmiller v. Dover (2005)

References

Agostini v. Felton, 522 U.S. 803 (1997).
Board of Education of the Westside Community Schools v. Mergens, 496 U.S. 226 (1990).
Edwards v. Aguillard, 482 U.S. 578 (1987).
Elk Grove Unified School District v. Newdow, 542 U.S. 961 (2004).
Engel v. Vitale, 370 U.S. 421 (1962).
Equal Access Act, 20 U.S.C.A. Section 4071 (1984).
Everson v. Board of Ed. of the Township of Ewing, 330 U.S. 1 (1947).
Grove v. Mead School District No. 534, 753 F.2d 1528 (1985).

Kitzmiller v. Dover, 400 F.Supp. 2d 707 (2005)
Lee v. Weisman, 505 U.S. 577 (1992).
Lemon v. Kurtzman, 403 U.S. 602 (1971).
Lynch v. Donnelly 462 U.S. 1104 (1984).
Santa Fe Independent School District v. Doe, 530 U.S. 290 (2000).
U.S. Const., amend. I (1791).
Wallace v. Jaffree, 472 U.S. 38 (1985).
West Virginia v. Barnette, 319 U.S. 624 (1943).

Additional Resources

Alexander, K., & Alexander, M. D. (2009). *American public school law* (7th ed.). Belmont, CA: Wadsworth. (SEE Chapter 5)

Fischer, L., Schimmel, D., & Stellman, L. (2010). *Teachers and the law* (8th ed.). Boston: Allyn and Bacon. (SEE Chapter 11)

Russo, C. (2004). *Reutter's the law of public education* (5th ed.). New York: Foundation Press. (SEE Chapter 2)

Thomas, S., Cambron-McCabe, N., & McCarthy, M. (2009). *Public school law: Teachers, and students' rights* (6th ed.). Boston: Allyn and Bacon. (SEE Chapter 2)

Underwood, J., & Webb, L. D. (2006). *School law for teachers.* Upper Saddle River, NJ: Pearson. (SEE Chapter 6)

Student Records 9

*The Family Educational
Rights and Privacy Act*

BACKGROUND ON THE ISSUE

In 1974, Congress passed the Family Educational Rights and Privacy Act
(also know as FERPA, 2000, or the Buckley Amendment) to clarify who
may and may not see student records. Congress passed the Act because of
problems in the use of student records, especially the tendency of schools
to provide outsiders with access to the records but to deny access to students and their parents.

The establishment of student records was originally a progressive
development that enabled teachers, counselors, and administrators to have
information about the "whole child," not just about grades and subjects
studied. But, the custom of allowing prospective employers, police, and
other outsiders to see the records that were barred to parents led to abuses.
For example, one mother was told that she had no right to see records that
resulted in her son being transferred to a class for the mentally retarded.
And a father, who was told by teachers that his son needed psychological
treatment, had to get a court order to see all of his son's records.
Furthermore, before FERPA was passed, most parents had little knowledge
of what was in their children's records or how they were used, and the
secrecy surrounding school records made it difficult for parents to assess
their accuracy or to challenge erroneous information in the records.

Thus, the goal of FERPA was to correct these problems. However,
some educators felt that the Act would cause more harm than good:
Teachers wouldn't put anything critical in the records because they feared
being sued for libel, and some administrators saw the Act as another
unfunded mandate requiring unnecessary procedures and paperwork. In
view of these concerns, this lesson clarifies what FERPA does and does not
require and some of its consequences.

Activator

Motivator

Ask teachers individually whether they think the following statements about FERPA in Table 9.1 are true, false, or they don't know. The principal may want to formally or informally tally the totals for each case.

7 min

Table 9.1 Student Records Hypothetical Cases

Student Records Hypothetical Cases	True or False		
Case 1. In order for teachers to have access to all of their students' records, they must have permission from the principal (or his designee) or a parent or guardian of the student.	True	False	Don't Know
Case 2. In order for a noncustodial parent to have access to his or her child's records, this person must have permission from the parent who has legal custody.	True	False	Don't Know
Case 3. If parents believe that something in their child's records is misleading, the parents have the right to a hearing to present their evidence and to challenge anything they believe is inaccurate.	True	False	Don't Know
Case 4. Parents must be notified every year of their rights under FERPA.	True	False	Don't Know
Case 5. A parent's consent is not required before schools share information from student records to protect the health or safety of the student or others.	True	False	Don't Know
Case 6. Parents have the right to see teacher's personal notes about their children.	True	False	Don't Know

paper copies

Student Records Hypothetical Cases	True or False		
Case 7. FERPA prohibits teachers from giving recommendations about their students to prospective employers over the phone without parental permission.	True	False	Don't Know
Case 8. Teachers can be sued for defamation for critical comments they put in a student's records if the negative statements cause economic harm.	True	False	Don't Know
Case 9. FERPA gives parents the right to file complaints with the U.S. Department of Education for failures to comply with the Act.	True	False	Don't Know

Rationale

Objectives

3 min

Rationale

Issues of student privacy abound in the public school classroom. Teachers need a better understanding of how to confront these legal issues as they arise.

Objectives

Post and/or state the following objectives for the lesson plan:

1. Teacher will be able to discuss the main features of the Family Educational Rights and Privacy Act (2000).

2. Teachers will be able to explain how the Act applies to teachers, students, and parents.

The Law

FERPA has five important features. It is important for the principal to disseminate the information about these five features to teachers. Divide teachers into groups of four. Ask each group to read through all five features (provide groups with a handout).

15 min

THE FIVE FEATURES OF FERPA

paper copies

1. The Right to Be Informed

The Act requires school districts to inform parents of their rights under the Act each year. This includes the right to be informed about the kinds and locations of education records maintained by the school and the officials responsible for them. Usually, this information is included in a school's student handbook. FERPA also requires schools to effectively notify parents whose primary language is not English of their rights under the Act.

2. Protects Confidentiality

FERPA protects the confidentiality of student records by preventing disclosure of personally identifiable information to outsiders without prior written consent of the parent. The consent must be signed, dated, and include the specific records to be disclosed, the purpose and the individual or group to whom the disclosure may be made. Schools must keep a file of all requests for access, including who made the request and why.

3. The Right of Access

FERPA guarantees parents the right to inspect and review the educational records of their children. This includes the right to receive an explanation or interpretation of the records if requested. Schools must comply with a parent's request to inspect records "within a reasonable time, but in no case more than 45 days after the request" (*Code of Federal Regulations,* Title 34, Part 99, 2004). Either parent (including a noncustodial parent) has the right to inspect their child's records unless prohibited by a legal document or court order.

Education Records. Education records include any information maintained by a school (or a person acting for a school) that is directly related to a current student, regardless of whether the record is in handwriting, print, tape, or computer file. The information may be in a teacher's or principal's desk as well as in an official file. However, FERPA (2000) does not give parents the right to see the personal notes of teachers, counselors, or administrators if these notes are used only as a "personal memory aid" and are not shared with any other individual except a substitute teacher.

Consent Not Needed. There are several *exceptions* where student records can be shared without parental consent. For example, prior consent is not required when education records are shared (1) with teachers, other school staff, and administrators in the district who have *"legitimate educational interests";* (2) with officials of another school in which the student seeks to enroll (provided parents are notified); (3) with individuals for whom the information is needed "to protect the health or safety of the student or other individuals"; (4) pursuant to a court order; and (5) in connection with financial aid for which a student has applied (FERPA, 2000). The Act requires each school district to adopt a policy specifying which school personnel have a legitimate educational interest in accessing student records. In addition, FERPA was amended in 1994 to explicitly allow schools to share information with teachers about disciplinary action taken against a student for conduct that posed a significant risk to any member of the school community.

Schools also have the option of sharing *directory information* from students' education records without a parent's consent. Directory information includes such facts as a student's name, address, e-mail address, phone number, date and place of birth, dates of attendance, awards received, and photographs. Before releasing such information, a school needs to try to notify parents of what facts it considers directory information and parents' right to refuse to release the information. A school may release information about former students without trying to notify them.

4. The Right to Challenge

The Act establishes procedures through which parents can challenge a student record they believe is "inaccurate or misleading or violates the privacy or other rights of the student" (FERPA, 2000). In such a case, parents first should request that the school amend the record. If the school refuses, it must advise the parents of their right to a hearing where they must be given an opportunity to present their evidence and may be represented by counsel at their own expense. The school must make its decision in writing, based solely on the hearing, and include the reasons and evidence to support its decision—which is final. If the school decides the information is correct, it must inform parents of "the right to place in the education records of the student a statement... setting forth any reasons for disagreeing with the decision" of the school (FERPA, 2000). The statement must be maintained by the school as part of the student's record; if the contested part of the record is disclosed to anyone, the parent's explanation must also be disclosed. This procedure includes the right to challenge an incorrectly recorded grade, but it does not give parents the right to contest whether the teacher should have given a higher grade.

5. The Right to File Complaints

FERPA gives parents the right to file complaints with the U.S. Department of Education concerning failures to comply with the Act. The *Family Policy Compliance Office* of the Department has been established to "investigate, process, and review violations and complaints." After receiving a complaint, the Office notifies the school, and the school has an opportunity to respond. After its investigation, the Office sends its findings to the complainant and the school. If there has been a violation, the Office indicates the steps the school must take. If the school does not comply, a review board could terminate federal education funds.

Over the years, the Office has received thousands of complaints, and about 80% have been resolved informally. Furthermore, there have been over 1,000 formal investigations, but in no case has a review board terminated federal funds for noncompliance. Moreover, individuals cannot sue for violations; only the Department of Education has authority to compel compliance. In addition to enforcing FERPA, the Office staff will consult with teachers and administrators by letter or phone to answer questions concerning the Act and its application in specific school situations.

In addition to their rights under FERPA, students in special education have additional rights concerning their records under IDEA (the Individuals with Disabilities Education Act). Because special-education services often involve sensitive personal information, IDEA requires staff who use such information to receive training about confidentiality requirements. Although FERPA allows schools to destroy student records at any time (except when there is a request to inspect them), IDEA requires schools to maintain IEPs (individual educational programs) and evaluations for at least three years to document compliance (for more on IDEA, see Chapter 3).

Application

Content to Practice

20 min

Assign each member within the groups a role: a defender, a prosecutor, a jury member, and a judge. Then, ask the groups to revisit the hypothetical cases used to begin the lesson. Give the defenders and the prosecutors a few minutes to make arguments for or against the hypothetical cases. The jury can then weigh in regarding who may have made the most convincing argument. Finally, the judge will reveal the answer (provided by the principal; see Table 9.2).

Table 9.2 FERPA Scenarios

paper copies

HTTP://WWW.CORWIN.COM/TEACHINGLAW

True or False
1. **False.** FERPA does not require that teachers get permission from an administrator or parent before accessing their students' records. Instead, the Act requires each school district to adopt a policy indicating which school personnel have a "legitimate educational interest" in seeing student records. Teachers certainly have such an interest. If there are schools that don't include teachers among those having a legitimate educational interest in viewing the records of students they teach or advise, this is the fault of the school district, not the Act.
2. **False.** Custodial parents do not have authority to prohibit noncustodial parents from accessing their children's records. On the contrary, according to FERPA, noncustodial parents have the same right to access their children's records as custodial parents unless such access is prohibited by a legal document or court order. As one judge wrote, schools should make educational information "available to both parents of every child fortunate enough to have two parents interested in his welfare" (*Page v. Rotterdam-Mohonasen Central School,* 1981).
3. **True.** FERPA gives parents the right to a hearing to challenge any of their children's school records they believe are inaccurate or misleading. Even if the hearing officer concludes that the challenged records are not inaccurate or misleading, parents still have the right to place a statement as part of the disputed record about why they disagree with the hearing officer's decision.
4. **True.** FERPA requires that parents be notified each year about their rights under the Act, including their right to be informed about the kinds of student records kept by the school and how they can review those records.

(Continued)

(Continued)

paper copies

True or False
5. **True.** A parent's consent is not required before the school can share information from student records with anyone if, in the judgment of school officials, the information is needed to protect the health or safety of the student or other individuals.
6. **False.** Parents do not have the right to see the personal notes of teachers, counselors, or administrators if these notes are only used as a personal memory aid and are not shared with anyone except a substitute teacher.
7. It depends on the facts of the case. FERPA only applies to student records. Therefore, if a teacher gives a recommendation (verbally or in writing) that is not based on information in the student's school records, FERPA does not require parental permission. But, if the recommendation is based on the student's records, then prior parental permission is clearly required.
8. **False,** if the information is true. Truth is a defense to charges of defamation. Therefore, even in the unlikely event that critical or negative comments about a student's behavior in school caused economic harm, they would not be grounds for a defamation suit if true.
9. **True.** The U.S. Department of Education has established the Family Policy Compliance Office to investigate complaints from parents (or teachers) about alleged failure to comply with FERPA. Most complaints are about misunderstandings or misinterpretations of the Act and can be resolved informally. Where this is not possible and a school does not comply with the Act, the Office can order compliance.

Assessment

5 min

For the ticket out the door in this lesson, ask teachers to list the five features of FERPA on a 3" × 5" card. On the way out of the meeting, the principal can trade cards; that is, teachers hand in their 3" × 5" card and, in turn, receive a card (see Table 9.3) that summarized the five features.

Table 9.3	FERPA Summary Card

1. *Inform.* FERPA requires schools to inform parents of their rights under the Act each year.

2. *Inspect.* It gives parents the right to inspect and review the educational records of their children.

3. *Challenge.* It provides procedures that allow parents to challenge records they believe are incorrect or misleading.

4. *Confidential.* It prohibits disclosure of personally identifiable student records to outsiders without parental permission.

5. *Complain.* It gives parents the right to file complaints with the Department of Education if they believe that there have been failures to comply with the Act.

FAQ

10 min

As time permits, you may add some of these additional questions to the follow-up discussion.

1. What schools are required to comply with FERPA?

All public and private schools and educational agencies that receive federal education funds, either directly or indirectly.

2. Who can assert their rights under FERPA?

Only parents or guardians can assert their children's right of access and consent until the children become 18 years old or begin attending a postsecondary school. After this, these rights can *only* be asserted by the student.

3. Can students waive their right of access?

Yes. Individuals who apply to a postsecondary institution may waive their right to inspect letters of recommendation. Although institutions may not require such waivers, they may request them. These waivers must be signed by the individual student rather than their parents.

4. Does FERPA apply to information about students that is not recorded?

No. Therefore, the Act does not prohibit teachers or administrators from disclosing information about students that is not recorded. However, sharing unrecorded *confidential* information with persons who have no need to know is usually unprofessional and unethical, might violate state privacy laws, and would be a valid reason for disciplinary action.

5. Can parents sue schools for violating their FERPA rights?

No. FERPA does not give parents the right to sue schools for violating their rights. The Act is only enforceable by the Department of Education, which can withhold federal funds from schools that have a policy or practice of releasing student records in violation of FERPA. However, some parents might still be able to sue schools where *state* laws prohibit disclosure of student records.

6. Is a student's class work or homework protected by FERPA?

It may not be. In a 2002 U.S. Supreme Court decision (*Owasso Independent School District v. Falvo*, 2002), Kristja Falvo objected to the practice of her children's teacher who had students exchange papers, grade them, and call out the scores, which the teacher then entered in a grade book. Mrs. Falvo believed this violated FERPA (2000). But, the Supreme Court disagreed and ruled that the grade did not become an educational record until it was recorded in the teacher's grade book. According to the Court, if all class work were considered an educational record protected by FERPA, this would impose a substantial burden on teachers and would make it more difficult for them to give students immediate feedback.

**Resource
Material**

Relevant Quotes

*The plain meaning of the language in FERPA sets forth what educational
agencies or institutions must do and not do in order to be eligible for federal
funds. They must not have a policy which denies or prevents parents from
having access to their children's educational records. . . . In addition,
FERPA requires that the educational agencies or institutions establish
appropriate procedures allowing parents access to the records upon
request. . . . [FERPA, 2000] is intended to give them [parents] the
opportunity to challenge and to correct—or at least enter an explanatory
statement—inaccurate, misleading, or inappropriate information about
them which may be in their files and which may contribute, or have
contributed to an important decision made about them by the institution.*

—Belanger v. Nashua School District (1994)

*While legal custody may be in one or both of the parents, the fact that it is
placed in one does not necessarily terminate the role of the other as a
psychological guardian . . . [FERPA provides] that funds should not be
available to educational agencies which deny to parents the right to inspect
and review the educational records of their children. The regulations
implementing the act allow inspection by either parent, without regard to
custody, unless such access is barred by State law, court order or legally
binding instrument. . . . Educators and school districts are charged with the
duty to act in the best educational interests of the children committed to their
care. Although it may cause some inconvenience, those interests dictate that
educational information be made available to both parents of every school
child fortunate enough to have two parents interested in his welfare.*

—Page v. Rotterdam-Mohonasen Central School District (1981)

*Under FERPA, schools and educational agencies receiving federal
assistance must comply with certain conditions. One condition specified in
the Act is that sensitive information about students may not be released
without parental consent. . . . [The parent's] construction of the term*

"educational records" to cover student homework or classroom work would impose substantial burdens on teachers across the country. . . . Even assuming a teacher's grade book is an educational record . . . the grades on student papers would not be covered under FERPA at least until the teacher has collected them and recorded them in his or her grade book.

—Owasso Independent School District v. Falvo (2002)

Excluded from FERPA's protections are records relating to an individual who is employed by an educational agency. . . . Although a [teacher's] file may contain "embarrassing or confidential information," the public interest in learning whether those who teach young children are qualified clearly outweighs her limited right to disclosure privacy.

—Klein Independent School District v. Mattox (1987)

Materials

3" × 5" cards

References

Belanger v. Nashua School District, 856 F.Supp. 40 (1994).

FERPA is found at Title 20, Section 1232g, *United States Code Annotated* (2000). Regulations for implementing the Act are in the *Code of Federal Regulations* Title 34, Part 99 (2004).

Individuals with Disabilities Education Act, 20 U.S.C. sec. 1400 (2004).

Klein Independent School District v. Mattox, 830 F.2d 576 (1987).

Owasso Independent School District v. Falvo, 534 U.S. 426 (2002).

Page v. Rotterdam-Mohonasen Central School District, 441 N.Y.S.2d 323 (1981).

Additional Resources

Alexander, K., & Alexander, M. D. (2009). *American public school law* (7th ed.). Belmont, CA: Wadsworth. (SEE Chapter 12)

Family Policy Compliance Office, U.S. Department of Education, 400 Maryland Avenue, S.W., Washington, D.C. 20202, (202) 260-3887

Fischer, L., Schimmel, D., & Stellman, L. (2010). *Teachers and the law* (8th ed.). Boston: Allyn and Bacon. (SEE Chapter 18)

Russo, C. (2004). *Reutter's the law of public education* (5th ed.). New York: Foundation Press. (SEE Chapter 13)

Thomas, S., Cambron-McCabe, N., & McCarthy, M. (2009). *Public school law: Teacher' and student' rights* (6th ed.). Boston: Allyn and Bacon. (SEE Chapter 3)

Underwood, J., & Webb, L. D. (2006). *School law for teachers.* Upper Saddle River, NJ: Pearson. (SEE Chapter 7)

Abuse and Neglect 10

BACKGROUND ON THE ISSUE

Teachers will likely confront situations where they suspect that one of their students has been abused or neglected. In these situations, teachers are required to report their suspicions to the appropriate authority. In addition to their legal obligations, teachers are expected to react sensitively and appropriately when a student discloses abuse. Knowing the signs of abuse and neglect, understanding one's responsibilities, and learning appropriate ways of responding to children who disclose abuse are an important part of being a well-prepared teacher. This lesson plan discusses teachers' legal obligations to report child abuse and neglect as well as how to detect and respond to abuse. In doing so, the lesson plan notes that different states have different standards of reporting.

Activator

Motivator

10 min

In small groups, teachers will have five minutes to discuss the following scenario.

> *A student approaches you (a teacher) stating that her stepdad beat her with an extension cord because she would not pick up her toys and refused to listen. The student is worried that if this gets reported, he will beat her again. Should the teacher report this suspected abuse and to whom? If not, why not?*

The principal will guide the teachers to always err on the side of reporting. This case clearly needs to be reported. However, many cases of abuse and neglect are more problematic and nuanced. This will be a good lead in to the rationale and objective for this lesson.

Rationale

Objectives

3 min

Rationale

Over 3.3 million reports were made to state child-protective agencies in 2008. Sadly, the National Child Abuse and Neglect Data System found that 1,530 children died in 2006 because of injuries related to abuse and neglect (Children's Bureau, 2006). Teachers are in a position to help prevent abuse and neglect. In fact, teachers are considered *mandatory* reporters and must report suspected abuse and neglect.

Objectives

Post and/or state the following objectives for the lesson plan:

1. Teachers will be able to describe the reporting requirements for abuse or neglect cases.
2. Teachers will be able to recall the protections against defamation if no abuse is found.
3. Teachers will be better able to identify cases of abuse and neglect.

The Law

12 min

The aim in this section is to help teachers understand how laws define abuse and neglect, how to identify cases of abuse and neglect, and when to report such cases. The principal should ask teachers to read the sections on pages 163–165 (Definitions, Reporting, and Identifying Abuse and Neglect). Next, lead a short discussion of these elements. Finally, hand out Table 10.1 to discuss strategies for talking with students about these issues.

Table 10.1	Talking With Students About Abuse or Neglect

Take the child seriously, remain calm and reassuring, find a private place to talk, and position yourself at the child's eye level. Children who disclose abuse are likely to feel anxious and unsure of whether or not they will be believed. Giving the child a sense of comfort and control will facilitate disclosure.

Speak on the child's level, listen intently, use minimal prompts, and respond with the language that the child uses. Using general prompts, such as "Tell me what happened," allows the child to retain control of the situation and reveal only as much information as he or she feels comfortable sharing. In addition, responding using the child's chosen vocabulary helps to ensure that the child's credibility is not damaged; when children use language that does not sound like an ordinary part of their vocabulary, they are often disbelieved.

Obtain only the information necessary to make a report. It is likely that the child will need to repeat the same information to investigators and/or social service workers. Minimizing the extent to which a child must relive painful experiences is important.

Be responsive to the child's feelings while reassuring him or her that the abuse is not his fault, that you are willing to help, and that he or she is not alone.

Tell the truth. Let the child know about the process that you must follow, and do not make false promises.

Thank the child for confiding in you. Let the child know that confiding in you may have been difficult, but it was the right thing to do. Also, inform the child that this information must be reported to the proper authorities.

Adapted from The Association for Childhood International's Resource for Teachers (Austin, 2000).

DEFINITIONS OF ABUSE AND NEGLECT

Federal law defines *child abuse and neglect* as "Any recent act or failure to act on the part of a parent or caretaker which results in death, serious physical or emotional harm, sexual abuse or exploitation; or an act or failure to act which presents an imminent risk of serious harm" (see the Federal Child Abuse Prevention and Treatment Act, 2003). Although this federal law sets a minimum standard, each state then provides its own definitions of abuse and neglect and procedures for reporting. For example, Alaska's law defines abuse and neglect as "the physical injury or neglect, mental injury, sexual abuse, sexual exploitation, or maltreatment of a child under age 18 by a person under circumstances that indicate that the child's health or welfare is harmed or threatened" (Alaska Statues, 2009).

State laws generally provide greater definition than the federal law, and they elaborate on the different forms of child abuse (e.g., sexual abuse, emotional abuse, abandonment). Unlike the federal law, which offers guidance, state laws are used to enforce child-protection procedures. Due to the varying information within each state's law, teachers should consult the laws of their particular state.

In addition to state laws, individual school districts have also adopted policies focused on abuse and neglect. A sample school-district policy from Lexington, Massachusetts, reads, "All LPS [Lexington public school] employees who have reasonable cause or suspicion to believe that a child is suffering physical or emotional injury resulting from abuse or neglect shall report such a belief to the appropriate authority, according to the LPS *Child Abuse and Neglect Reporting Procedures*" (Lexington School Committee Policy, 2003).

REPORTING ABUSE AND NEGLECT

Most state laws outline the procedures for making a report of child abuse or neglect. A typical procedure would be for the superintendent and/or school board to establish reporting procedures in accordance with the law of the state. Whereas some school districts require the teacher to report the alleged abuse to a school counselor or school psychologist, other districts require teachers to report the abuse directly to the child protective services agency. Also, in most states, there are penalties when teachers fail to report abuse or neglect that they knew or should have known about. For example, in Indiana, a teacher who fails to report suspected abuse or neglect may be confined up to 180 days and incur a $1,000 fine (Children's Law Center of Indiana, 2003). Teachers are also required to report the abuse in a timely manner. New Jersey's law is fairly typical in stating, "any person having reasonable cause to believe that a child has been subjected to child abuse or acts of child abuse *shall report the same immediately*" (New Jersey Statutes Annotated 9:6–8.10, 2009, emphasis added).

The Seventh Circuit Court of Appeals upheld a school district's decision to discipline a school psychologist who failed to report suspected child abuse in a timely manner (*Pesce v. J. Sterling Morton High School,* 1987). There are also penalties for falsely reporting child abuse. However, if a report is made in *good faith,* the teacher will not be penalized even if an investigation determines that no abuse took place.

After an investigation, the appropriate agency might require several alternatives. For example, the family might receive services, there could be a court proceeding, or, in the worst cases, the child might be placed in foster care. Ultimately, there could be a termination of parental rights.

IDENTIFYING ABUSE AND NEGLECT

Whether a student directly discloses abuse, or a teacher has reason to suspect that a child in her class is being neglected, teachers need to know what to look for and how to respond. The National Clearinghouse on Child Abuse and Neglect Information (n.d.) has developed resources to assist reporters in identifying child abuse and neglect. Additionally, several scholars have written on the topic (see References and Additional Resources at the end of this chapter).

As noted by Saisan, Jaffe-Gill, and Segal (2008), physical abuse can manifest itself clearly in unexplained or patterned injuries, particularly those that seem age-inappropriate or have a pattern, as though made by a hand or belt. However, when there are no physical marks to indicate abuse—as in emotional or sexual abuse—behavioral signs or caregiver actions may help a teacher recognize an abusive situation. Behavioral signs can include fearfulness or shyness, inappropriate knowledge of or interest in sexual activity, destructive behavior, or extreme aggressiveness or passivity. Of course, children could be exhibiting these types of behaviors for many other reasons; identifying abuse and neglect is indeed complex. Thus, when a child does not have physical marks but exhibits one or more of these behavioral signs, it would be prudent to discuss your observations with a specialist (e.g., the school psychologist). In addition to children exhibiting signs of abuse or neglect, the guardian or caregiver may show certain signs as well, including a lack of care for the child or a lack of interaction with the child, or they may seem particularly controlling or protective.

Disclosure of abuse can come in many forms. Children may confide in a teacher directly, disclose abuse to a friend, or reveal information through written or pictorial work. When this happens, teachers have an opportunity to provide comfort and support in addition to meeting their legal obligations. The guidelines in Table 10.1 (see page 163), adapted from the Association for Childhood International's resource for teachers (Austin, 2000), should assist teachers who need to respond to the disclosure of abuse and neglect.

Alternative

Invite a local protective services worker or court official to discuss the identification of abuse and neglect and the procedures that are followed upon receiving a report. Provide the person with the lesson plan (especially objectives and readings) prior to the professional development session.

Application

Content to Practice

20 min

In small groups, the teachers will discuss whether they should alert a school or childcare agency official about suspected child abuse. The principal will choose three to four of the scenarios in Table 10.2 for the teachers to discuss.

Table 10.2	Abuse and Neglect Scenarios

HTTP://WWW.CORWIN.COM/TEACHIN

Scenario 1

One day, you're reading a book to your third-grade class. The story talks about a family cooking dinner together. As they prepare the meal, they gather items from the refrigerator. After the story is over, one of your students, Sarah, comes up to you and asks more about the "refrigerator." She says that she doesn't have one of those at home. As you ask her more questions, you discover that her family does not even have electricity at home. You've noticed that Sarah has come to school dirty, but until now, you had no suspicions that she was not cared for at home.

Question

Do you report this to a school or childcare agency official as possible abuse or neglect?

Scenario 2

As you're on lunch duty, you see a fourth-grade student, Jack, hiding in the back of the lunchroom. When you approach him, you notice that he is rummaging through the garbage and is holding a half-eaten sandwich. When you ask him what he is doing, he appears embarrassed, throws the sandwich in the trash, says, "Nothing," and hurries off. You tell his teacher, Mrs. Mallory, what you witnessed. She says, "Yeah, I caught him doing that last week. The little sneak!" She then talks about what a problem Jack has been this year. He never has his homework done and is often teased by the other children because he smells. When you ask Mrs. Mallory, who has been teaching for about 15 years, whether you should report the incident to the school social worker because perhaps Jack was rummaging for food because he doesn't get enough to eat at home, Mrs. Mallory looks at you like you have three heads. She says, "Wow, you really *are* naive! If you went running to the social worker every time something like this happened, you'd never get any work done!"

Question

Do you report this to a school or childcare agency official as possible abuse or neglect?

Scenario 3

Larry is a first-grade student in your class. He was also in your class last year but was held back. Last winter, there were many days when it was below freezing that he came to school without a winter coat. Today, it was 10 degrees and Larry came to school without socks, in short sleeves, and his hair was still wet. You know his family is facing hard times ever since his dad was laid off from work. At the same time, you're worried that he is not being cared for properly. The other day, he mentioned that because he has to share a single bed with his two brothers, he usually ends up sleeping in the bathtub.

Question

Do you report this to a school or childcare agency official as possible abuse or neglect?

Scenario 4

You teach kindergarten. The children are given free time to play when they finish their morning work. During this time, Abby is playing with one of the dolls. When she thinks no one is looking, she moves toward a corner, puts the doll down her pants, and begins humping the doll. You have never seen this behavior before.

Question

Do you report this to the school or childcare agency official as possible abuse or neglect?

Scenario 5

Sixteen-year-old Heather has been a quiet student. One day, her nose starts to bleed in class, and some of the other students inexplicably laugh at this. When you approach her and start to write up a pass for her to go to the nurse's office, she tells you that her parents are Christian Scientists, and it is against the beliefs of her religion to seek medical help. The student further explains that she has not seen a doctor since she was born and that when she had a seizure last year, her parents simply prayed for her recovery.

Question

Do you report this to the school or childcare agency official as possible abuse or neglect?

Scenario 6

One day, you accidentally brush against 14-year-old Shelly as you walk by her, and she jumps. You reach out to steady her by taking hold of her arm, and she flinches and looks nervous. After class, when the students are leaving, you casually apologize to Shelly for startling her. She waits until the classroom clears and then blurts out that she knows a girl who gets hit by her dad and that her friend's situation is making her jumpy.

Question

Do you report this to the school or childcare agency official as possible abuse or neglect?

The principal can use Table 10.3 to lead discussions about each scenario. This can also make a good handout.

| Table 10.3 | Answers to Abuse and Neglect Hypothetical Scenarios |

Scenario	Principal Guidance
1 (Report)	It is always best to err on the side of caution. A teacher should report to and allow officials from child protective services to investigate. One of the outcomes may be additional resources for the family.
2 (Report)	
3 (Report)	
4 (Report)	Touching dolls sexually is one of the warning signs in identifying abuse. However, kindergarten students are also curious about bodies. In this case, it is more than touching, and it would be prudent to call child protective services.
5 (Report)	Parents have a right to freely exercise their religion without government interference, but courts have permitted intervention when the parents' behavior puts the safety of the child at risk. In some cases, courts have found it unacceptable for parents to neglect a child because of religious beliefs, and they have ordered medical treatment. These cases have come to be known as "religious-based medical neglect." Scenarios such as this one are difficult; however, it is always best to err on the side of caution and make a report.
6 (Observe)	Although one could err on the side of caution and report, it may also be reasonable to continue to observe this student's behavior.

Assessment

5 min

Ask teachers individually to create a plan of action in regard to how they will modify their interaction with students regarding suspected abuse or neglect. Specifically, ask teachers to write common scenarios of abuse and neglect they might encounter and what they will do about it. (Note: Do not allow teachers to discuss real cases in their classrooms, so individual students are not identified.)

| Figure 10.1 | Abuse and Neglect Assessment |

FAQ

10 min

As time permits, you may add some of these additional questions to the follow up discussion.

1. **How can I find more information about my particular state's law regarding abuse and neglect?**
   The Child Welfare Information Gateway allows individuals to search each state's abuse and neglect laws. The list of state laws can be found at www.childwelfare.gov/systemwide/laws_policies/state.

2. If a child tells a school counselor about abuse in confidence, must the counselor disclose this information?

Yes. Teachers and counselors have a duty to report all suspected child abuse or neglect even if it was conveyed in confidence.

3. Are teachers considered mandatory reporters?

Yes. All teachers are considered mandatory reporters because of their closeness with students. In addition to teachers, the following other groups of people are usually considered mandatory reporters: doctors and healthcare providers, social workers, childcare providers, and law enforcement. The Children's Bureau reported that in 2006, teachers reported more cases of abuse and neglect than any other group of professionals.

4. Will a reporter's identity ever be disclosed?

Most likely not. All states require that abuse and neglect records be kept confidential. Currently, 39 states specifically prohibit the disclosure of the reporter to the alleged perpetrator. However, there are some circumstances where the reporter's name could be identified, for example, if a case proceeded to trial, and witnesses needed to be identified.

5. What should you do if your superior does not believe there is abuse or neglect and refuses to report it to the appropriate agency?

In this situation, a teacher must still report the suspicion to the local child protective service agency.

6. Must you be convinced about the abuse before reporting?

No. Although the precise language varies among states, a teacher should report if she or he has a *reasonable suspicion* of child abuse. New Jersey's law is fairly typical in stating: "any person having reasonable cause to believe that a child has been subjected to child abuse or acts of child abuse shall report the same immediately" (New Jersey Statute Annotated 9:6–8.10).

7. Can a teacher be penalized for reporting abuse that is not substantiated?

No. All states provide teachers with immunity if the report was made in good faith.

Relevant Quotes

Schoolteachers, school officials, and school authorities have a special responsibility to protect those children committed to their care and control. School officials and school authorities, in particular, have special relationships with their teachers and direct control of the environment in which their teachers and students interact. When these persons are informed that one of their schoolchildren has been sexually abused by one of their teachers, they should readily appreciate that all of their schoolchildren are in danger. In no other context would we give even a second thought to the proposition that a school board has an obligation to deal with an instrumentality of harm to one of its students at school for the benefit of all of its students.

—Yates v. Mansfield Board of Education (2004)

The purpose and intent of the statutory scheme is to encourage the prompt reporting of all suspected cases of child abuse. Blanketing mandated reporters with a presumption of good faith and imposing civil liability for a breach of the mandated duty to report further encourage the prompt reporting of suspected abuse. A determination that liability for a failure to report is dependent upon whether the charges are founded or whether the child abuse petition is ultimately sustained would contravene the statutory purpose of encouraging prompt reporting, and we decline to follow that approach. We conclude that a mandated reporter is obligated to report suspected cases of child sexual abuse based upon facts and circumstances within the knowledge of the reporter at the time the abuse is suspected and may be held liable for a breach of that duty even though it might ultimately be determined that the abuse was not committed or allowed to have been committed by a "person legally responsible" for the child.

—Kimberly v. Bradford Central School (1996)

References

Alaska Statues 47.17.290 (2009).

Austin, J. S. (2000). *When a child discloses sexual abuse: Immediate and appropriate teacher responses.* Olney, MD: Association for Childhood Education

International. Retrieved March 29, 2009, from http://www.acei.org/TR%20Child%20Abuse.pdf

Children's Bureau. (2006). *Summary: Child maltreatment 2006.* Washington, DC: U.S. Department of Health and Human Services, Administration for Children & Families. Retrieved March 28, 2009, from http://www.acf.hhs.gov/programs/cb/pubs/cm06/summary.htm

Children's Law Center of Indiana. (2003). *A duty to report child abuse.* Retrieved February 24, 2010, from http://www.kidsvoicein.org/documents/Chins/Duty/1.pdf

Child Welfare Information Gateway. (n.d.). *Homepage.* Retrieved March, 25, 2009, from http://www.childwelfare.gov/can/defining/federal.cfm

Federal Child Abuse Prevention and Treatment Act (CAPTA) (42 U.S.C.A. §5106g), as amended by the Keeping Children and Families Safe Act of 2003.

Kimberly v. Bradford, 649 N.Y.S.2d (N.Y. App. 1996).

Lexington School Committee Policy. (2003). *Child abuse and neglect policy.* Retrieved February 24, 2010, from http://lps.lexingtonma.org/about/childabuse(rev).pdf

National Clearinghouse on Child Abuse and Neglect Information. (n.d.). http://www.nsvrc.org/organizations/67

New Jersey Statutes Annotated 9:6–8.10 (2009).

Pesce v. J. Sterling Morton High School, 830 F.2d 789 (1987).

Saisan, J., Jaffe-Gill, E., & Segal, J. (2008). *Child abuse and neglect: Warning signs of abuse and how to report it.* Retrieved March 31, 2009, from http://www.helpguide.org/mental/child_abuse_physical_emotional_sexual_neglect.htm

Additional Resources

Alexander, K., & Alexander, M. D. (2009). *American public school law* (7th ed.). Belmont, CA: Wadsworth. (SEE Chapter 9)

Child Abuse Prevention and Treatment Act, 42 U.S.C. § 5101 *et seq.*

Fischer, L., Schimmel, D., & Stellman, L. (2010). *Teachers and the law* (8th ed.). Boston: Allyn and Bacon. (SEE Chapter 7)

Russo, C. (2004). *Reutter's the law of public education* (5th ed.). New York: Foundation Press. (SEE Chapter 13)

Strachan-Peterson, M., Durfee, M., & Coulter, K. (Eds.). (2003). *Child abuse and neglect: Guidelines for identification, assessment, and case management.* Los Angeles, CA: Volcano Press.

Thomas, S., Cambron-McCabe, N., & McCarthy, M. (2009). *Public school law: Teacher' and student' rights* (6th ed.). Boston: Allyn and Bacon. (SEE Chapter 8)

Underwood, J., & Webb, L. D. (2006). *School law for teachers.* Upper Saddle River, NJ: Pearson. (SEE Chapter 5)

Conclusion

The Principal as Chief Law Instructor: Living the Role

The lack of school-law knowledge can be yet another diversion in the long line of distractions for school educators. How could we help remedy this situation? We set about this process with two important convictions: first, that the principal is uniquely positioned and highly capable of being the school's chief instructional officer; second, that educators can be armed with the legal knowledge and skills that would help the important work of teaching and learning. As a result of these beliefs, we created a set of legal lesson plans that give principals the tools they need to be conscious, informed, and effective law teachers for their staff.

Continuing to neglect the issue of legal illiteracy in schools will lead to costs, both emotional and financial. School principals have the authority and opportunity to design and implement inservice professional development programs in this critical area, which has been largely neglected in teacher preparation programs. Sadly, most teachers gain their information and misinformation from colleagues who are similarly uninformed and misinformed. That is why it is so important for principals to correct this misinformation and provide their teachers with the basic knowledge they need to be legally literate. Armed with this knowledge, teachers will be unlikely to make the common legal mistakes described in these lessons, such as putting unprofessional information on Facebook or a personal blog, unintentionally violating students' constitutional rights, or hesitating to discipline students because of unfounded fears of liability. Thus, as a result of these lessons, both principals and teachers will be able to commit their time and talent to their primary job—providing quality education for their students.

Appendices

Appendix A

Conducting Legal Research

The purpose of this appendix is to assist principals and teachers with finding free legal resources (e.g., case law, statutory law) on the Web. The following Web sites are easy to use and a great resource for school-law information.

FINDLAW

FindLaw is a free site that contains U.S. Supreme Court decisions, federal laws, federal decisions, and other state resources. The site also has a specific link to school law topics.

- To find the Education Law Section: go to www.findlaw.com.
- Click on View More underneath the Individual Issues link on the right-hand side. Click on Education Law under the Other Topics link.

This site has a frequently-asked-questions page, specifically related to school legal issues, an overview of special education law, and forms. You may also ask legal questions via e-mail.

- To find the Cases and Laws Section, go to www.findlaw.com/casecode.

In this section, you may search by case name, topic, federal laws, federal decisions, and you can find various state resources.

CORNELL UNIVERSITY LAW SCHOOL LEGAL INFORMATION INSTITUTE (LII)

LII is a free legal database that has U.S. Supreme Court decisions, federal laws, federal decisions, and other state resources.

- To find this site, go to www.law.cornell.edu.

In this Web site, principals and teachers can use various search terms to find federal laws, U.S. Supreme Court opinions, and some federal and state court opinions.

NATIONAL SCHOOL BOARDS ASSOCIATION (NSBA)

NSBA is a not-for-profit organization comprising state associations of school boards. The organization represents the interests of school boards in school legal matters. Also, NSBA distributes a free weekly e-mail that highlights the most recent lawsuits filed. Students, as well as principals and teachers, are encouraged to subscribe to the NSBA's Legal Clips via e-mail at http://www.nsba.org/legalclips.

- The organization's Web site address is www.nsba.org/default .aspx.

EDUCATION WEEK'S SCHOOL-LAW BLOG

Education Week has an excellent school-law blog containing postings about cases, current events, and other items of interest.

- This particular blog can be found at blogs.edweek.org/edweek/ school_law.

This blog also links to other good school-law blogs, including *At the School House Gate, Principal's Policy Blog* (NASSP), the *EdJurist Accord,* and the *Special Education Law Blog.*

OYEZ

At this site, you may listen to actual U.S. Supreme arguments. Also available at this site is interesting information about U.S. Supreme Court justices, including a virtual tour of Justice Kennedy's chambers.

- The address for this site is www.oyez.org.

GOOGLE

Searching on Google will also locate a variety of information; however, be careful that the information is not dated (and, therefore, no longer good law) or inaccurate. Google may be used to find state statutes. For example, by typing the "state name" and "code," most state statutes can be found.

Appendix B

Constitutional Sources of Education Law

The three most applicable amendments to school-law cases include the following.

- **First Amendment (Religion, Speech, Press, Assembly, Petition)**

  Congress shall make no law respecting an establishment of religion, or prohibiting the free exercise thereof; or abridging the freedom of speech, or of the press; or the right of the people peaceably to assemble, and to petition the government for a redress of grievances.

- **Fourth Amendment (Search and Seizure)**

  The right of the people to be secure in their persons, houses, papers, and effects, against unreasonable searches and seizures, shall not be violated, and no warrants shall issue, but upon probable cause, supported by oath or affirmation, and particularly describing the place to be searched, and the persons or things to be seized.

- **Fourteenth Amendment (Due Process, Equal Protection)**

  Section 1. All persons born or naturalized in the United States, and subject to the jurisdiction thereof, are citizens of the United States and of the state wherein they reside. No state shall make or enforce any law which shall abridge the privileges or immunities of citizens of the United States; nor shall any state deprive any person of life, liberty, or property, without due process of law; nor deny to any person within its jurisdiction the equal protection of the laws.

Appendix C

The Court System

STATE COURTS

The state court system has three levels: trial courts (usually called circuit, superior, or district courts), appeals courts, and a state supreme court. States use different terminology to describe the three levels. Plaintiffs may file their lawsuits in state court or in federal court (if there is a federal issue involved).

FEDERAL COURTS

The federal court system also has three levels: district courts, circuit courts of appeals, and the U.S. Supreme Court.

DISTRICT COURTS

There are 94 district courts in the United States. Decisions from a district court can be reviewed in the court of appeals for the circuit in which the district is included. For example, if a federal district court case from Indiana is appealed, the case would be heard in the Seventh Circuit Court of Appeals. All federal judges have lifetime appointments.

COURTS OF APPEALS

There are 13 courts of appeals. The courts of appeals usually hear and decide cases in three-judge panels. The courts of appeals are listed below.

- *First Circuit:* Maine, Massachusetts, New Hampshire, Puerto Rico, Rhode Island

- *Second Circuit:* Connecticut, New York, Vermont
- *Third Circuit:* Delaware, New Jersey, Pennsylvania, Virgin Islands
- *Fourth Circuit:* Maryland, North Carolina, South Carolina, Virginia, West Virginia
- *Fifth Circuit:* District of Canal Zone, Louisiana, Mississippi, Texas
- *Sixth Circuit:* Kentucky, Michigan, Ohio, Tennessee
- *Seventh Circuit:* Illinois, Indiana, Wisconsin
- *Eighth Circuit:* Arkansas, Iowa, Minnesota, Missouri, Nebraska, North Dakota, South Dakota
- *Ninth Circuit:* Alaska, Arizona, California, Guam, Hawaii, Idaho, Montana, Nevada, Northern Mariana Islands, Oregon, Washington
- *Tenth Circuit:* Colorado, Kansas, New Mexico, Oklahoma, Utah, Wyoming
- *Eleventh Circuit:* Alabama, Florida, Georgia
- *Federal Circuit:* All federal judicial decisions
- *District of Columbia:* District of Columbia

THE U.S. SUPREME COURT

This court has nine justices, one of whom is the Chief Justice. The Supreme Court sits in Washington, D.C. The Supreme Court hears less than five percent of the cases it is asked to hear each year. As of June 2010, the members of the Court are John Roberts (Chief Justice), John Paul Stevens, Samuel Alito, Ruth Bader Ginsburg, Clarence Thomas, Antonin Scalia, Stephen Breyer, Sonia Sotomayor, and Anthony Kennedy. The Supreme Court justices have lifetime appointments.

Appendix D

Additional Resources

Dunklee, D. R., & Shoop, R. J. (2006). *The principal's quick-reference guide to school law: Reducing liability, litigation, and other potential legal tangles* (2nd ed.). Thousand Oaks, CA: Corwin.

Essex, N. L. (2009). *The 200 most frequently asked legal questions for educators.* Thousand Oaks, CA: Corwin.

Shoop, R. J., & Dunklee, D. R. (2006). *Anatomy of a lawsuit: What every education leader should know about legal actions.* Thousand Oaks, CA: Corwin.

Streshly, W. A., Walsh, J., & Frase L. E. (2002). *Avoiding legal hassles: What school administrators really need to know.* Thousand Oaks, CA: Corwin.

Swofford, S., & Longo, P. M. (2003). *Essentials of school law.* Thousand Oaks, CA: Corwin.

Index

CORWIN
A SAGE Company

The Corwin logo—a raven striding across an open book—represents the union of courage and learning. Corwin is committed to improving education for all learners by publishing books and other professional development resources for those serving the field of PreK–12 education. By providing practical, hands-on materials, Corwin continues to carry out the promise of its motto: **"Helping Educators Do Their Work Better."**